The WHEEL *of* JUSTICE

MR. CLIFFORD UBANI

ISBN: 978-1-7339038-0-6

The Wheel of Justice is a story about Mr. and Mrs. Clifford Ubani and family and his experience with the US justice system; the current flaws and matters relating to injustice, discriminations, right to counsel of choice and court proceedings. The story tells of how he struggled through life in a society that appears to operate two sets of laws, one that depends on the color of one skin as African-American family of Nigerian descent.

Equal justice under the law is not merely a caption on the facade of the Supreme Court building, it is perhaps the most inspiring ideal of our society. It is one of the ends for which our entire legal system exists... it is fundamental that justice should be the same, in substance and availability, without regard for economic status

LEWIS POWEL JR.

TABLE OF CONTENTS

CHAPTER ONE

THE HUMBLE BEGINNING

There is but one blasphemy, and that is injustice.
ROBERT INGERSOLL

I learned while growing up that the court is the last hope of the common man. Before you support or kick against that, you should ask yourself this, is there actual justice in the world? You would be surprised what answer I found to that question. A piece of advice before I tell you what answer I found, never you find yourself on the wrong side of the law, and never you underestimate the little details about the law. When it comes to the law, make sure you cross all your T's and dot all your I's. Just a little mistake and you would be sorry for the rest of your life. At every point in time, the law remains your best ally, and if you find someone who can help you interpret it well enough, then you are a free man. This opinion has always been my perception about the justice system of the United States—the home of the free and brave.

Before I let you have a taste of my experience with the justice system, I'd like to walk you through my journey from my birth home, Nigeria.

Born in Ohanze Isiahia, Aba in Abia State, Nigeria in the late fifties, life never gave me the chance to enjoy some fatherly love. My father, Mr. Ngwakwe William Ubani, was a hardworking man who never got the chance to nurture his children or watch my two siblings and me grow up to become the fulfilment of his dream. He passed on in 1968 while I was only 10 years old. It was quite an ugly time for my family and me who needed some close fatherly care at the time. We were still trying to shake off the losses of the Nigerian civil war at the time. My mother felt like the world was over for her. In the middle of a civil war, she had to lose the one person she needed most at the time. We mourned our dead and picked up our broken souls as we continued to find survival in the middle of the war. I had just started elementary school when the tragedy struck. It was part of my mother' pains and also part of my pains as well. We worried about how I would go through school and eventually finish considering the current condition of things in my family. For me, my education had already come to an end right before it started. As a little boy, I had dreams of getting my education to the highest level or at least up to the university. However, this ill-timed incident made me imagine the possibility of that dream happening. I had thoughts racing through my head. On several occasions, I contemplated if I would have to forget about formal education and learn a trade or acquire a skill. Something had to be done. This I knew. There was no way I was going to accept sit idle at home, especially at my tender age. Honestly, I had my mind prepared for the worse. If it meant I had to stop schooling to meet up with the needs of the family, I was willing to pay that price. However, my mother always had something cooking; she was never known to give up easily, people said she was always ahead of her peers, and I thought so too.

By and large after the war, there was relative peace, we settled down again and then, we felt the hollow my father's death had left us. There were lots of things to be put in place, and we needed all the support we could get, but that period was a wrong time to even go to other people for support. Everyone was busy counting their losses. My mother used to own business prior to the civil war, but she lost it during the war. She might have lost the physical business and some of her customers, but she never lost that entrepreneurial instinct. As a typical Igbo woman from a traditional African society, she had learned over the years to be industrious. Thanks to her upbringing, she was taught to be hardworking as well. It was time she employed some of the lessons she had learned from her late mother, my grandmother. Mrs. Eliza U. Ngwakwe, my mother, single- handedly raised my two siblings and me. I bet you can imagine what it meant for a woman to raise three children all by herself.

Destiny is a good thing to accept when it's going your way. When it isn't, don't call it destiny; call it injustice, treachery, or simple bad luck.
JOSEPH HELLER

27 July, 2009 was the beginning of my ordeal. That day brought to us one of the worst experiences we have ever had as a family. Our life-altering experience with the Justice System as a family started around July 27, 2009. We were at home the evening of the said day when members of the Medicare Strike Force Team (OIG, FBI) and others stormed my resident like they were cramping down on a terrorist group. The sight was one of those you see in the movies when a terrorist kingpin has just been made. My resident in Houston, Texas that evening was greeted with a frightening sight. The vehicles, SUVs and police vans surrounded my house throwing my wife and children into a panic. Of course, I had been expecting them within that period, but not a raid. They swooped my resident like I was

some terrorist on a watch list. My neighbors wondered what was going on. The neighborhood was thrown into a frenzy. It was an ugly sight. The kids in the neighborhood ran inside and even adults scrammed to safety. It was obvious where they were going. Everyone could see that it was the residence of the Ubanis that was being raided by the FBI. I told my wife and kids to stay calm that all would be well. They couldn't help panicking as more agents hopped down from their vehicles with rifles taking their positions like they were on some assault mission. I don't blame my wife and kids for feeling terrified, nor the neighbors for freaking out. Even I too was taken aback by the sight before us. I first heard sirens and wheels pulling over around my house. I couldn't quite make out the scene at first. Then, I started hearing sounds of people running into their residents and parents calling out to their children, my last girl opened the curtain and peeked through.

"Dad."

"What is it, girl?"

"Dad, you need to see this."

I could sense the sudden fear in her flustered voice as she voiced those words. My entire family ran to the window to behold the sight. From the window, I could see the officer in charge of the case step out of his car and gave some orders. I could only interpret by the movements of the other agents that he had asked them not to allow anyone close to or out of the building. As he walked towards my front door, I quickly called my lawyer and informed him of the sight before me. He told me not to worry; and that I should follow them quietly. He didn't need to tell me that, I was in the force and I knew the drill. There was no way I was going to resist arrest, not while my family was close. While he walked closer to the door, two other officers joined him. They banged on my door.

"Get inside, guys. And nobody should make any move," I said to my children as I went to answer the door.

My children remained still; they stood there looking at the door like they were prepared to beat up whoever came in through the door. As I held the doorknob, I looked back and noticed their stillness.

"Honey, take the kids to their rooms."

I opened the door and there they were, scary-looking, armed federal agents.

"Good evening Mr. Clifford Ubani. Federal Agent Ross." The senior officer that gave the order greeted and showed me his badge.

"Good evening, officer Ross. Officers."

We are here to bring you in and to search your premises. He said showing me an arrest warrant. I looked at the court order for my arrest and a search warrant. "Please, if you don't mind coming with me while the officers search the house."

"Of course, officers." I obliged them and turned around to my family: my wife was holding back the tears in front of the kids; by now, they were already crying.

"Honey, I'll be fine, take care of the kids," I said as I stepped out with the officer in charge.

I remembered my mother, mamma Eliza, as she was fondly called and how that she became my role model. She started rebuilding her local business again after the civil war. She wanted us to be self-sufficient with her local business. Indeed, she was a thriving local entrepreneur. She was the most hardworking woman I ever met. She had only one goal—to help her family succeed. Well, she did her best to make sure we got there. Memories of her spurred me up and before long, I was thinking like her. Her local business had sustained my siblings and me, but it wasn't enough to get me to the height I was aiming. So, I started thinking of what I could do to support her and my siblings the more. I was my mother's son, and I carried my father's blood. At the tender age of 11, I already started helping myself, running errands for neighbors and family members and making some savings from that. For a young boy my age, the monies I was making was encouraging. I learned to be humble and opportunistic. I was raised to be respectful and humble; I used that to gain attention and with my hardworking spirit, I was able to get people commit some little responsibilities to me.

The more the people trusted you, the more they gave you little jobs to do. To a lot of kids, the errands were like punishments, but for me, it was a real-time job. I made money from some change I got and sometimes the tips I got from the uncles and aunties who sent me. I also looked for places I could do real job, like supply water for a building project or convey goods from farms to the market. These jobs came in handy and allowed me make some savings.

Another tragedy struck me in 1972, one that broke my wings and had me crawling on my knees. My mother, Mama Eliza, my heroin, lost her life in 1972, precisely 4 years after my father had died. She lost her life to typhoid fever. Apparently, she has been living with malaria for a long time, we saw the symptoms but couldn't do much at the time. There were days when she broke down due to malaria, but she would tell us not to worry that she would be fine. She would eventually get better after taking some drugs, either herbal medicines or the most common Paracetamol. What we didn't know was that she never really got better. She had accumulated malaria in her and as at the time she died, there was really nothing we could do about it. She fell sick and as usual we started giving her the regular herbs. Some of her friends came and helped us prepare the herbs, my uncle did what he could do, but she needed a special attention—that we couldn't afford. All we did was apply the herbs and prayed, hoping that she would be fine. Sadly, she never did. Her condition got worse with the passing of each day. As hours turned into days and then weeks, I watched my mother's body gradually fray. I knew she wasn't going to make it; I was only hoping God would heal her.

Sadly, it was one of those times God decided to let his permissive will be done. My mother eventually died and my aunts and uncles tried to hide it from my siblings and me. I felt it, I knew my mother had died, I was only waiting for them to break the news. I noticed from the way my uncles and aunts suddenly became more caring and attentive to us. I knew they were only trying to sympathize with us—more like to "prepare" us for the sad news coming. Four days passed after mother died before they eventually told us. It broke my siblings down, but I had already cried my eyes out the nights before they broke the news. I wasn't the oldest son, but I was very close to my mother and had a strong heart. I pulled myself together and acted all-strong. I remember my mom once telling me to always be a man and never show signs of weakness before any of my relatives. I put up that boldness and walked out of the room. I went to sit under an almond tree and sobbed. I had been solely responsible for myself all the while my mother was sick. I let my older brother look after our only sister while I contributed my small quota. My hopes that my mother would recover and at least, help take some of the responsibilities were crashed against the wall by the cold hands of death. I guess I was about becoming a man sooner than I thought. Thanks to her, I had learned quite a few lessons about life and survival. While I was under the tree, my thoughts began racing wide and wild. I found myself asking me whether I was ready to take up the responsibility waiting for me. I wasn't the first son, but I felt like I had so much to do. I was filled with so much sense of responsibility. I questioned myself if I could actually grow into that young boy my mother always wanted me to become. The answers were not straight jacketed. I was filled with fear, disappointment, sadness, anger and bitterness.

I didn't really know what next I was going to do. I was still under the almond tree when my uncle walked up to me and encouraged me, he told me to follow him inside, but I refused. He insisted and I followed him out of respect for his age. I really didn't want to see my siblings in their bereaved and helpless state; neither did I want them to see my fear and bitterness. Somehow, I found the courage to face them.

I went inside the room with my uncle and immediately hugged my siblings. We held each other and gave way to the piled-up tears of our saddened and wailing hearts. They allowed us some moments before pulling us away from each other. I was really broken on the inside of me. That night was the longest in our family's history. I would close my eyes to rest and would open it at the sound of my brother's sobs. I would go closer to comfort him. Sometimes he stopped and at other times he just sobbed the more. My younger sister was even worse. She cried all through the night and there was nothing either I or any of our relatives was able to do to make her stop. We couldn't sleep.

The following morning, my older brother and I went with my uncles and aunties to carry my mother's belongings that were still in the hospital. I asked that I be shown my mother's corpse, but they maintained a refusal, adding that I would see her corpse on the day of her burial. It was more painful for me that they didn't let me see my mother's corpse. They told me according to tradition, only the *opara* (first son) was allowed to see the corpse before the burial.

Law catches flies, but let hornets go free.

As I stepped out through the door with the officers who had come for my arrest, my family could no longer swallow the cries that were now choking them. They let out a billow of weepings as my wife pulled them together. Two of the officers entered the house while two others followed. I was escorted to the vehicle and sat in between two officers at the back seat of an SUV. From there I could see the four officers coming out through my front door. My wife and kids stood at the entrance of my house while they watched as I was driven out of the resident. I was driven to the FBI office and kept in a holding room. The cell was typical of one those cells you see in the movies. I never imagined in my entire life that I would be in such a place. It was different from the cells I stayed to interrogate criminals or suspects during my time with the force. After a while, an officer dressed in a fine black jacket and a blue neck tie walked into the holding room. He was neatly dressed and had a shiny black pair of shoes on. That is what it looks like when you are a well fed, you just have to look good. They were well paid and often got extra tips when they cracked cases—like mine. He sat down in front of me and smiled. I could see the hidden mischief in those curved lips of his. He introduced himself and I barely took note of his name. I was only interested in what I was being arrested for. It was in that room that I learnt I had been indicted on multiple counts of health-care fraud and conspiracy resulting from my activity on official capacity as CFO in Family Healthcare Group, Inc., a company I co-owned with a business partner from June 2006 to October 2, 2008.

I was dazed by the charges that were leveled against me. My mind raced in thoughts trying to figure out how all that happened. I questioned every journey that I had been through, traced every path I walked since I got to Houston. Even though he gave me the dates my supposed crimes were committed, I was still trying to ascertain how it happened. I couldn't find the answers within me, I just sat down numb. It was unlike me. As a former officer of the United State, I was familiar with the processes involved in interrogation and all of that. There were questions I needed to ask, as a matter of fact, I really wanted to ask them, but, instead, I just sat down and waited for my lawyer. I was very certain I would defend myself in the court of law. In such cases, I have learned from experience, never argue with federal agents. You can only argue with them in the court of law. I was certain the charges would be dropped after a fair hearing in the court of law. Sadly, as a citizen of the United States, I was not given the opportunity to appear before the grand jury or even to know in details the allegations leveled against my company and me.

I was unjustly and arbitrarily rushed, then got indicted by the grand jury without regard to its own OIG internal self- guards in that it accused me. I was expecting that the OIG would be smart enough to understand what it meant to go against its own standards and deny a citizen his right. But that didn't mean anything to the agency. They blatantly failed or should I say ignored to honor their own internal rules, self-guards and procedures established by them to assist the health care industry to comply with the Nation's fraud and abuse laws and to educate the public about fraudulent scheme so they can protect themselves and report suspicious activities. All of those standards and practices meant nothing to them.

I tried several times to make them see that they were wrong and contravening their own rules. I preached the sermon of my rights but it only fell on deaf ears. They had this all figured out—they planned it. I could see where this was coming from. The rush to conclusion without any interest to uncover the truth and the way they neatly made the narrative of my involvement left me with only one conclusion—the system was bias. They were on us because maybe because we were the owners of the business and we were a minority African-Americans of Nigerian descent. My attorney did all he could to secure a fair hearing, but these guys were good at making sure the truth stayed buried when they wanted it covered up. In such situation that I was in, they were the only ones that could make the truth resurface. Even my White attorney told me while we were in his office in Downtown, Houston that if I was to be a White man from Beaumont, Texas area I wouldn't be here.

CHAPTER TWO

THE STRUGGLE THROUGH SCHOOL

My life has had a lot of stitches long before those officers rounded my home like that of some terrorist, yet I was a citizen of the United States, only of Nigerian descent.

Days turned to weeks and my mother was finally laid to rest. I was in elementary four at the time. The day of the funeral was another day I couldn't hold myself. I wept so bitterly that I lost my voice, my siblings too were uncontrollable. We were all still very young for the tragedy that had befallen us. We were surrounded by sympathizers, but none of their words meant anything to my siblings and me.

"Take care. Be strong. Stop crying. Take heart. It's well. etc." were the clichés echoing from all directions of our small sitting room. I saw faces I had never seen before and was introduced to people I never knew existed. Some of them were my father's friends who only showed up after their late friend's wife had passed on. Some were my mother's customers and business associates. Some were un-familiar faces from her town's meeting. And others were the distant relatives whose names we only heard on the lips of our parents. The more I saw them was the more I wept and could only wish they had showed up before my mother died. I imagined the kind of support they would have rendered, given the little effort we made to keep her alive. What hurt me the most was that a lot of these persons who had come to condole with us were indebted to either my late father or my late mother and some of them were well to do and could have been able to help us. The crowd that never seemed to stop coming only made things worse for my siblings and me. Their presence and words only reminded us so much of our mother.

By the time the day was over, we had received enough 'sorry' to compete with the sands on the shores. They echoed in our heads and made things worse. The silence that greeted the room the days after sent me a strong message that we were on our own. My uncles and aunts stayed back for some days and left us with some money. Some of the guests who came to mourn with us also left us with some monies, food items and other gifts. We decided to live off what was left behind, but I knew it wasn't going to serve.

You can't keep tearing your hearts out, you have to become a man and take care of yourself and your siblings, I thought to myself. I called my older brother and told him it was time we helped ourselves the way our parents had taught us. He saw reasons with me and also said he had similar thoughts in his head. He told me that he wasn't expecting me to start going to work and making money, but he was expecting me to stop crying and start living the life our late parents had left us. The earnings from my errand runs were no longer enough to put food on the table of three orphans left to fend for themselves. I needed something more lucrative and rewarding. I tried my hands on a lot of things. I worked on people's farms, fetched firewood for families and also split the firewood. But they still didn't serve the means. I started skipping school to be able to meet up with the tasks I was paid to do. My grades were taking a consistent nosedive. I had to sit myself down and talk to myself. I pictured if my parents would be proud that I was abandoning education to be able to meet up with the needs of the family. My mother had always taught me that there was always a better option and, often times, they are the ones we never take. I searched my head for ideas on how I would be able to take care of myself and help my older brother take care of my younger sister. I had two years to finish primary school, but I still had a whole six years to wrap up basic education. At this time, my older brother was already done with primary school and was already working to support my sister and me. He was willing to sacrifice his education for ours, which he did.

"Brother, what if we do houseboy and housegirl for people?" My sister suggested with a soft and uncertain voice to my older brother and me.

I looked at her sharply and saw the sense in what she was saying. My brother looked at me as if buying into her suggestion. She was only 10 years old at that time. I thought about what she said, she actually meant for us to work as housekeepers in people's homes and get paid for it. She was too young for that path, plus, I doubted if my older brother would let me do it. My brother insisted that he should be the only one to do that, that we should focus on our studies. I didn't accept the bench he was about placing me. I suggested to him that we should do it differently. Eventually, we decided that we would not stay in people's houses, instead we would go early in the morning, clean the houses and do the necessary chores, go to school and come back in the evening to take care of what needed to be done. It worked out quite well for us—and for me, especially since I was already 14—they thought I was just the perfect age and would be better able to take care of things. There were families that hired my services out of pity after hearing my story. Two years later I was done with my primary education and had to start the processes of seeking admission into a secondary school. Well, it wasn't as difficult as I had imagined for it to be. I got the admission into our neighboring community's secondary school in 1974 and there continued the remaining part of my basic education. My community didn't have a secondary school, so the lot of us either went to the communities around us or to town—for those who could afford it there and had relatives, too. I also had relatives in town, but they never showed interest in my education nor those of my siblings, so we just counted them out of our plans for a support system.

It was quite tougher in secondary school than in the primary, but I soon got adapted to the system. I made a few friends and of course some others decided to be my foe. At this time, I had already gained the trust of some families and already had regular daily schedule with the families. My only problem was I had to walk 4 kilometers from my community to my school to and fro every day. And it wasn't just me, there were other kids too from my community. That became a problem for me. I was waking up earlier so that I could meet up with the families and also with school. Somehow, I was always late to school and always got either a corporal punishment or got myself flogged by either the teachers or prefects on duty. My brother became my father, encouraging me each time I told him of my ordeal in school. I explained to some of the teachers and the senior students what I was going through and some of them decided to help me out of sheer. They did help me, but only on their duty days. I still got either the punishment of clearing grasses or cleaning out dirty classes or getting flogged on the other days. Sometimes I would weep at the treatments and at other times, I manned up and acted all cool.

My first year in secondary school was the toughest. The bullies, the extra workloads, the new environment, the long walks and the consistent labor works all contributed to the problem I already had. Exam periods were the worse for me. I get back home exhausted every day and still had to do some chores at the different homes I have been hired. I barely had time to study, even when I managed to save some time to study, I always ended up sleeping off while studying. However, I never relented, I kept on studying for the short periods of time I could. They say, little drops of water make a mighty ocean; that was the case for me. I made sure I studied every day for at least an hour. Those little efforts paid off. My first term result in JSS 1 wasn't so bad, even though I knew I could have done better if I had enough time and resources. We've always been known as highflyers in our academics, but the months following our mother's death brought us down the basest rung of the academic ladder. It was expected given the fact that we had to take care of things ourselves. At the end of my first year in secondary school, I knew I had to do something about the distance. I spoke with some of my teachers who were close to me and they decided to help me. They told me it would be wise to consider working for families within my school's host community. That meant I would have to move temporarily to the residents of any of the families that decided to hire my services as a housekeeper and are willing to let me live with them at the same time.

That wasn't an easy decision for me. I shared the idea with my older brother. At first, he was reluctant to buy into the idea while my younger sister insisted that I considered the option. It took us a whole year to consider the option. When I was finally ready, I went to a particular family that accepted my help. Their terms were pretty simple and direct. I was only going to be employed for a year because the family just had a baby and they needed someone to help out with the chores. For me, it was easy because I was an active participant in the upbringing of my younger sibling. I had once helped my aunt look after her kids so I pretty much understood what it was like working in a house of a family with a newborn. My only fear was the short period the job would last. It meant I would have to look for another family that would be willing to house me and still pay me for the work I do. I didn't have a choice at the time, I just had to accept the job with the family and still keep my eyes open for other families with longer periods and better working terms and, of course, better payment. I took the job and started working.

My first one month was easy but riddled with thoughts and memories about my family. These people I worked for— they were kind to me—they were good people. They showed me so much understanding and love that I wished the contract was for a longer period. I started making more savings since I was no longer spending more on food and other things. My academic performance improved and I was on my way to competing with the top members of my class again. My school had shortage of teachers, so I was virtually passing through almost the same set of teachers from my first year to where I was. Some of my teachers who had taught me before noticed the differences in my current academic performance and that of the previous years. They were impressed and encouraged me to keep it up. The teachers who had encouraged me to get a job within my school's host community were more impressed and happy I made the decision and was finally stepping up my potential.

I had enough time for my chores, homework and personal studies. The family I was working for were kind enough to let me go visit my siblings every Sunday. That was one thing I was eternally grateful to them for. On some weekends, my siblings would borrow my cousin's bicycle and ride down to come see me. They were always welcomed each time they came and treated with same love I was enjoying. My younger sister was particularly fond of the baby and so were the baby and its mother. I had cordial relationship with the family; they took me as their own son. As my year of contract with the family went mid-way, I started feeling like I was going to miss them. I wished time would slow down and let me enjoy one of the things I've missed since my mother's passing—the authentic love of a mother. My madam's love and care couldn't replace my mother's, but it sure went a long way. I was never the type to fall sick quickly; people say I had a strong immune system. They were right, I was always the last to catch a contagious infection or disease. They said I inherited it from my grandfather. I never met the man, but if the things I heard about him were correct, then, I am grateful to be associated with such a man and thankful for leaving me with such a gift. One of the things I also benefitted from my employers is a better spiritual life. I've always been a Christian, my family has. But, we were never always that active in church, especially after my father's death. We even worked on Sundays just to be able to meet up with pressing needs. My mother taught us to love God and serve him from our hearts, but we were in a traditional society and fetishism prevailed. My madam made sure I became a devout catholic and ensured that I never missed mass, except I had to. I also transferred my religious beliefs to my siblings and they too loved it. My faith in God became stronger and I became spiritually wiser and it translated to my physical sense.

When the one year was finally complete, it was a sober moment for every member of the family. I had become part of the family but they needed to let me go, plus, they had also planned to move to the city which wasn't part of their earlier plan. My siblings came and helped us move their bags and luggage into a truck that they had hired. My boss got a better job in the city and was able to afford life in the city. They left my siblings and me some gifts including clothing and some money. It was a mixed feeling that day; first, we were happy for the gifts and clothing; but then the second thought of the fact that we would be missing a rare beautiful souls like my boss and his dear wife made us sad. I was introduced to another family to work with by my madam. However, at first, the family was unwilling to accept me because of the price. I had to go back home again and continue my senior secondary school walking from my own village to school. It was like starting all over again. Good thing it was only for a while. After the first term of my first year in senior secondary school, the family decided to take me in. I moved again to my school's host community and started all the adjustments again except for the school. The new family wasn't like my previous boss' and I didn't expect them to be. As a matter of fact, my former madam had told me not to compare any family I met with theirs. She told me if I wanted to carry out my job with ease and with less problems with my new boss, I should put her and her husband out of the mental picture. I took her advice and it paid off. I opened my mind to work with the new family and though it was challenging initially, I still managed to work with them. Although my time with them was also short lived, I got one good gift from them. We visited Ogbor-Hill in Aba for a function and there I met a young girl, Ezinne, about three years older than I. We got along and she shared with me her experience and I did mine. After that meeting with her, we became friends. Though she was younger than I, we were both in the same class.

I got another family to work with before the end of that year. I parted ways with the other family and moved to my new employers'. The new family had four children all within the ages of 3 and 10. Well, I felt the family was lazy and the parents were not helping the children take responsibility. There were always more jobs to be done in this new family but I adjusted quite easily. I was only a year and half from completing my secondary education and I wasn't willing to let anything stop me at that point. I took the hard way to life and it sure worked out for me. I was disappointed at the way my new boss was raising their children. They had little or no sense of responsibility.

At about the same age as they, I was already helping my parents with a lot. Even my younger sibling at this age did better. I guess it was all due to exposure their father's kind of exposure. He walked in the city with some foreign expatriates. He was away all Mondays through Fridays and only stayed in the village on weekends. He sometimes brought me gifts too from the city. I was only allowed to visit my family at home once in a month and my siblings were not allowed to come visit me. That was the part of the job that gave me a huge blow. I got used to it especially as they payed higher than the other families I had worked for.

During my final year in school, I had to register for the Senior School Certificate Examination. I had made enough savings to take care of that, but my boss decided to help with 70% of the money I needed for the examination. I registered and sat for the examination. As at 1980, I had successfully completed secondary education and was only awaiting results. I was anxious but I was also sure I wasn't going to fail.

Eventually, they were released and I checked for mine. I was so happy with what I made: four credits including mathematics and English, I made a B in Literature, Economics and Accounting and then an A in Agriculture and Commerce. My boss was so proud of me he instructed his children to imitate me. My teachers and friends were also happy, not to mention how glad my siblings were. I wrote to my former boss in the city about my results and he too sent his congratulations. He told me he would get back to me—what that meant I didn't know.

If I were to summarize how I completed my basic education after the deaths of my parents, I would say that I went through the remaining of my elementary and secondary school through self-help via domestic services to other families who could afford to pay and house me. I had a cousin who was a year older and three classes ahead. He was the closest family member I had asides my siblings. There were days he came visiting me and shared with me his plans of traveling abroad. He eventually did two years before I graduated from secondary school. He wrote to me while I was still in school that he got some connections through his father's colleague and that made it easier for him to travel. I envied him though, I was happy for him. Since I had a certificate, I knew I could now find better jobs and don't have to depend on other families anymore for support. I moved back to my home town and started looking for jobs. When I didn't get yet, I continued my domestic work with families but no longer full time. I had three different families I was working for. I did that as a temporal job. I lost contact with my friend Ezinne. We used to write each other, but three months after our final exams in secondary school, I didn't hear from her again. I felt bad but took it as one of those experiences. She remains as one to be remembered.

CHAPTER THREE

THE MEDICARE STRIKE FORCE TEAM

Laws are spider webs through which the big flies pass and the little ones get caught
HONORE DE BALZAC

L et me tell you something about those officers that stormed my home and took me away from my wife and kids. Well, they are called the Medical Strike Force Team, and you know what they do? You are about to find out.

The United States government is always very sensitive to health and they don't joke with the law. You break it, you pay. There are different agencies responsible for implementing the law. These agencies derive their powers from the constitutions and other laws that established them. In the United States, other than the military departments, the first Office of Inspector General was established by the Act of Congress in 1976 and it was under the Department of Health and Human Services. The aim of this is to fight waste, fraud and abuse in Medicare, Medicaid, and more than 100 other HHS programs with approximately 1,600 employees. The OIG performs audits, investigations, and evaluations, to establish policy recommendations for decision-makers and the public. Before major decisions are made, there must be a thorough investigation and report by the OIG to enable proper decision making. The reason behind this is that when decisions are to be made, there is enough information to validate the decision and policy and enough information to back up the policy. If a report is inconclusive, the policy would be placed on hold and the agency would be given more time to carry out a more thorough evaluation and submit a more authentic report. This is how the US functions from time to time. Before decisions are made in any sector at all, there must be enough information to back up the policy and decision otherwise the public will revolt and may even sue the agency responsible. To avoid public revolt and a possible failure of any policy at all, the US relies on effective and solid information before implementing.

In the US, there are 73 federal offices of inspector general, this is a significant increase since the statutory creation of the initial 12 offices by the Inspector General Act of 1978. The offices employ special agents – criminal investigators, often armed, and auditors. In addition, federal offices of inspectors general employ forensic auditors, evaluators, inspectors, administrative investigators, and a variety of other specialists. Each of these special agents has their defined responsibilities and jurisdictions, but they are all involved in common goals. Their activities include the detection and prevention of fraud, waste, abuse, and mismanagement of the government programs and operations with their parent organizations.

They carry out different investigations whether internal or external. When office investigation is internal, they target mainly government employees. When it is external, their targets are mostly grant recipients, contractors, or recipients of the various loans and subsidies offered through the thousands of federal domestic and foreign assistance programs. The Inspector General Reform Act of 2008

(IGRA) amended the 1978 act by increasing pay and various powers and creating the Council of the Inspectors General on Integrity and Efficiency (CIGE). This gave some of the agents more power and at the same time reduced the powers of some of the agents. Agents' activities were strictly monitored and reported to the necessary authorities. No agent was allowed to take actions beyond the limit that the law and constitution provided. Agents are not allowed to share information about their own program with agents from other programs except they had clearance to do so. Sometimes agents may need information from other agencies, before such is granted, the agency will have to clear with the authorities to verify the need for the information and sometimes, if the information in question is classified, the agency may not give it up to another agency unless it is very important. Healthcare information that falls under the Protected Health Information (PHI) can only be shared when necessary.

In practice, the Office of the Inspector General does not only investigate or carry out activities related to crime, the OIG also develops and distributes resources to assist the health care industry in its efforts to comply with the Nation's fraud and abused laws. They also organize conferences and trainings for the general public to educate them about fraudulent schemes so they can protect themselves and report suspicious activities. Since the commencement of this training procedure, we have seen a lot of physicians report and others serve some form of punishments. There were times when patients ignorantly reported physicians. There've been abuses of the privilege the OIG gave to the public to report fraudulent cases. The false report often given to the OIG by the public about physicians has raised concern in recent times.

In the recent past, the OIG has made an effort to pay more attention to hospitals and health care systems for Stark Law and Anti-Kickback Statute violations pertaining to the management of physician compensation arrangements. In 2015, a fraud alert was issued to publicize the OIG's intent to further regulate such non-compliance. This increased the awareness level of the public and physicians too became more careful and thorough with their modus operandi. In light of such efforts and consequent record-breaking settlements, healthcare experts have begun to call for the transition from paper-based physician time logging and contract management to automated solutions. In the US, a lot of laws regarding the healthcare sector seem to favor clients and patients more than it favors the physicians. This has made it a little difficult for some smaller firm to effectively carry out their job and it has also led to the merging of two smaller firms just to meet up with the demands of the law. When you are under investigation for the Stark Law and Anti-Kickback Statute violations, you are at the risk of a possible jail term. The Medicare Strike Force Team was responsible for carrying out arrest on physicians or healthcare practitioners that were found guilty. However, when you are arrested, you will get the chance to have a fair hearing in keeping with the constitutional rights of every US citizen. When you have been tried and found guilty, you will be sentenced to prison depending on the nature and extent of your crime. Serious offenders get more jail term and in some cases, you only get to pay some fine. In the US, so far, it has been difficult to walk away free from the net of the Medicare Strike Force Team. They were considered to be one of the most thorough agents in the OIG.

The Medicare Strike Force Team was not in existence since the OIG was established, it was recently founded in March, 2007. When it was created, it had its main aim as to prevent and combat health care fraud, waste, and abuse as a part effort to recover, generate and outsource fund to finance Affordable Healthcare otherwise known as Obama Care. A lot of people raised questions about the Obama care and how it would be paid for. This is America and you cannot come up with a policy and expect the American people to accept it hook, line and sinker. It doesn't work like that. After the administration was questioned about the cost of the program, the administration decided to show the American people how it would be able to pay for the program. Although there were still questions raised about the Obama Care, the response by the administration eased off a lot of tensions that initially arose when it was first announced. The program flagged off and it became a concern for health care practitioners. Every physician and hospitals in the United States started making adjustments to be able to accommodate the recent laws.

CHAPTER FOUR

THE BOY IS A MAN

After I graduated and starting looking for a better job, I always kept in touch with my first boss and his family. I also kept in touch with my cousin in

the US; he wrote to me every year, sometimes twice in a year. I was willing to join him over there, but I knew I needed money to make such a significant relocation. I eventually stopped working as a keeper of homes and instead took children on after-school lessons. It was more prestigious and rewarding than the housekeeping job. Although the money was still not enough, it was better than doing housekeeping as a young school leaver. I put in several applications to different organizations and firms, but none was willing to hire me. Through my first boss in the city, I secured my first real employment after Secondary school in the Nigerian Electric Power Authority (NEPA) in 1981, precisely eleven months after I graduated from secondary school. I was hired to work as a clerical staff with full clerical duties from administrative to accounting. It wasn't an easy one considering its tedious amount of workload, but I was willing to do my best to ensure that I delivered. The job sometimes was exciting and fun to do, at other times it was either stressful or too mind-numbing for its monotonous nature. There was always lots of paperwork to do, I was moving from one accounting process to the other, from one record to the other. The clerk before me didn't quite perform well in record-keeping. I spent the first six months arranging files and archives according to dates. I also made sure that the documents were arranged in their order of relative importance. My boss was impressed with my organization and recordkeeping skills.

"You're doing a great job here, boy," My boss said the first time he entered my small office.

"Thank you, sir. I couldn't leave them how they were."

My boss nodded and smile. He came close to me and pats me on my shoulders "well done, well done." He looked around the office and handed me a file. "Go through the content and bring the records concerned to my office before the end of tomorrow."

"Okay, sir," I answered as I collected the file from him and started going through it.

He left the office, and I could see the satisfaction written all over him. I quickly started looking for the files in question. They were easy to find given the way I had already arranged the office. I went to the years and searched by months. When I found them, I didn't just send the files to him. I waited until the following morning before delivering the records to his secretary as soon I got to the office that morning. I was always on time when it came to finding records and files, and when I couldn't find a file at all, it was apparent the file had either been misplaced by the previous clerk or was never in the office. One thing I also noticed was a forgery. Many documents had been tampered with; the previous clerk had been involved in some dirty businesses with other workers and customers. I knew it wouldn't be long until they approached with similar offers. In other to prevent such from happening I quickly exposed every compromised document to my boss, and he didn't hesitate to address them. Some persons were angry that I went straight to the boss and not the persons involved, others were happy that at least the shady deals that have been going on in the office would finally stop. That act alone discouraged those who would have brought shady deals to me. They knew I was a straight forward young man and I don't hesitate to report anyone who dares such to the branch manager. After I made the report, the manager instructed that every department submitted their record for cross-referencing. A supervisory team was set up, and they found many discrepancies in the records. The persons involved were either fired or queried. It sent a strong message to those involved and other colleagues. The accounts of customers involved were debited and made to pay for the months they tried to boycott.

I felt terrible for those who lost their jobs; it was as though I took away food from the tables of their innocent children. After speaking with my siblings about it, they told me not to feel bad, that I only did the right thing. I thought within myself that they were right. If I had ignored my findings, it would have bounced back to me. I would have put myself in conditions that would have likely cost me my job, plus, it was against all that I knew and I believed. Some of my friends said it was a test of my faith; they called it a temptation that would have opened a door for other temptations. They also said it was a good thing I didn't go to the persons involved prior; or else they would have either offered me some bribes or brought me into their league or even find a way to get rid of me from the office so that I don't expose them. I did my job diligently and with all humility that everyone in the office loved me, not everyone, most persons did. What came first to me was that I was doing my job as I ought to and my branch manager was always pleased? There were weekends he would invite me to his house and ask me to help him with some paper works. Those days were always fun for me. His wife would prepare me breakfast and lunch, and I also get extra money when I was going back home.

While I was working, I was planning on how to further my education. I never lost sight of that despite how much I was making. I had always wanted to be called a university graduate. This time I had my eyes on studying abroad and I did everything I could to keep that dream alive. I kept in touch with my cousin and also explored the opportunities my job as a clerk with the Nigerian Electric Power Authority (NEPA) gave me. I was acquiring the necessary papers one by one.

The most important thing I needed was already with me at the time. I had saved enough money after working for five years with the Nigerian Electric Power Authority (NEPA). I used the job also to acquire some documents and recommendations. The job paved way for me. After my second year with NEPA, I had made a decision that I'll work for five years before going back to school. My plans were either study at home or abroad, but my primary interest was always abroad.

I knew it would be easier studying in Nigeria, but I wanted a more prestigious certificate and a more educating and enlightening experience. So, I opted for education abroad. I worked with the Nigerian Electric Power Authority until December 20, 1986, when I applied for a study-leave to further my education. In my application, I didn't specify where I was going to study, but in my mind, I already knew I was going abroad. My application was not received with warmth. My boss would have loved to keep me in the office, but he understood why I was leaving; it was for something that would be of positive value to the team when I return. I got the leave and started making the final plans to travel abroad. I only told a few persons about my plans. I was waiting to be sure I was going abroad before telling more persons; I didn't want to be ignorant of my society. The fewer persons that knew, the more natural it was for me and the better. When I got my visa and traveling ticket, I finally told my boss at the NEPA office and a few more persons I felt needed to know. They were all both surprised and happy for me.

The night before the trip was a long one for my siblings and me. I tossed and turned on my bed, woke up several times before dawn. My older brother noticed I was barely sleeping; he advised me to try and get some sleep. I eventually did, but still woke up earlier than I should. I got up and had a bath and waited for dawn. My siblings had no choice but to wake up as well and prepare. They helped me carry my luggage to the park where I joined a bus heading to Lagos. I have visited Lagos once with my boss at NEPA; we went for a conference on power management and distribution. I was happy I would see the prestigious Centre of Excellency again, but my mind was fixed on Houston. I couldn't wait to get to Lagos and eventually get on a flight to the US. I imagined what the trip would look like from Lagos to Houston. I have never been on a plane before, I've heard a lot about flying; the plane crashes and the fear and also the fun. The take off some said is usually the most frightening, some said the landing is usually the most frightening while some conclude that flying is frightening. I couldn't wait to find that out myself. I got to Lagos late in the night. My flight was not until the following morning at 8 am. We were supposed to arrive Lagos at least 4 hours earlier than we did considering the time we left my home town. However, our vehicle broke down somewhere in Edo state, and we had to spend over three hours fixing it. By the time I got to Lagos, I was already too tired to do anything. I never knew traveling could be this exhausting. I could only take my bath, eat something substantial and collapsed on my bed. I decided I was going to get enough sleep that night; I didn't want to miss anything during the flight from Lagos to Houston.

I woke up the following morning and got prepared. I made sure I was at the airport before 8 am. I got to the airport precisely 35 minutes earlier. I sat down and fed my eyes, paying attention to everything my sight could capture. I was told to keep my ears open to the flight announcer, so I would know when my flight was ready. That was easy to do. I sat beside a lady who seemed older at the departure, she engaged me in some interesting conversation, and we were both heading the same direction.

"First time to fly?"

"Yes, mama," I replied nodding my head.

She smiled at me and received my hand. "I was like you once—nervous. I heard all the good and bad things about flying, and I was also afraid to fly. However, once we took off, everything was okay for me. It was an awesome experience and one to which I would like you to open your mind. Don't mind all the stories you've heard and read about flying."

Her words comforted me and made me somewhat relaxed. The truth is that I wasn't really scared of flying, I was just nervous, curious to know what it felt like. Our flight was delayed for another one hour. So, we just sat down and talked. I shared my story with her and told her why I was going to Houston. She sympathized with me and encouraged me. More importantly was the words she said to me about me.

"I am proud of you; the way you have become a man. Not many children would come out of such ordeal and still become successful and positively ambitious like you." Her words made my day, and they also taught me something: I have to keep up the hard work and even work harder. Just like the Holy Bible says, "To whom much is given, much is expected." I knew I had to do more.

CHAPTER FIVE

LIFE IN HOUSTON

*Once you start seeing injustice in one place, it is like taking off blinders
— you start seeing injustice in everywhere and how it is all connected.*

MARK AMES

I arrived in Houston, Texas in December 1986. Right there at the airport, mama's son came to pick her up. She helped me contacted my cousin who told us he

was on his way already. Mama introduced me to her son and left with me a means of reaching her. She also gave me twenty dollars and told me to call her when I was home with my cousin. I waited at the arrival for my cousin to come. He showed up later than he had initially told us, but there was nothing I could do. He apologized and gave his excuse which I never really paid attention to. I was enjoying the scenery at the airport. My only fear was the way the airport police kept on observing me and asking me questions. I also had a lot of other arrivals looking at me like there was something wrong about me. Well, I wasn't surprised at all with the way they were looking at me. It's Houston, Texas and it's December, a cold season and I was dressed like some guy from the streets of Lagos. Of course I was just coming from Lagos, but not from the streets. My cousin laughed at me when he saw I was not well covered for the weather. He had told me to dress up at least in thick clothing because of the cold weather, but somehow, I forgot that part of the letter and considering Aba and Lagos were hot at the time I left Nigeria.

He drove me in his car to his house. I couldn't help but turn my heads in different directions. There were so many things to feed my eyes on. My cousin just laughed at me each time I fooled myself. The buildings, the landscapes, the people and the serenity of the environment all contributed to my exclamations and surprises. The aesthetics appealed to my whole being. I got overly excited and surprised that at some point my cousin had to ask me to calm down so we don't get pulled over by the police and have ourselves arrested or embarrassed. That calmed me down but wasn't enough to keep me from looking around and smiling sheepishly at the beauties we drove past. We got to his apartment and I was again filled with surprise. He had quite a comfortable apartment, I wasn't really expecting less considering the fact that he had a good job and has been working for over three years. I stood at the entrance of his apartment and stared in awe at the beautiful apartment he has. It took him to come back and pull me inside the apartment. I couldn't help but walk around, admiring every detail I could find. Seeing the way I admired the room, my cousin decided to show me around the house. He showed me each room and showed me the most important things I needed to know at the time. It took me over half an hour to come out of my surprise. I was waiting for the rules and the lecture on how things worked in Houston. But he wasn't quick to address me; he wanted me to be fully settled in before taking me on a ride through the *modus operandi* of the *oyinbo* people. He showed me the shower, I quickly had my bath, got dressed and was ready to sleep. My cousin insisted that I ate something which I did.

After my shower, I started appreciating why I needed a cardigan. My cousin gave me a blanket that night to help me keep warm. I told my cousin about the elderly woman from the airport in Lagos and how she was helpful all through the flight and the twenty dollars she gave me. I had only 200 dollars as at the time I arrived Houston, but thanks to mama, I now have 220 dollars. I had my cousin call her that night and inform her I was home with him. She asked him to give me the phone, he did and we spoke for another six minutes before hanging up. My cousin gave her his house address and told her she was welcomed to visit.

"O boy, you just had yourself a mother in Houston." My cousin said sarcastically.

He might have joked with the statement, but he was right. The older woman so far has acted no less than a mother. From the airport in Lagos to the flight down to Houston and the call tonight, I saw nothing less than a mother. She brought to me memories of mine. I smiled and went to the room my cousin had shown me earlier. I was tired and didn't find it difficult to down myself in sleep. I knew I had a lot of things to learn, but that would have to wait until the following day, by that time I would have fully regained my energy from the whole stress of the journey. Flying from Lagos to Houston for over 13 hours after a stressful ride from Aba to Lagos the previous night wasn't easy. I woke up the following morning feeling so much better and stronger, the night was indeed peaceful. I survived the cold of my first night in Houston, and that meant I would survive the subsequent ones. I didn't wake quite early, it was unlike me to wake up later than 5 A.M. But I found myself waking up at past 7 A.M. That says how exhausted I was from the two-day journey. My cousin made me breakfast that morning and later in the day he started telling me about Houston. He told me most of the things he thought I needed to know and added that the rest I would find out myself. He already knew why I had come to Houston and though I expected him to have made some moves in that regards, he only made part arrangements. He told me he had gotten in touch with some of the schools and found out their requirements, cost and admission processes. I told him that I only had 220 dollars and I needed a job to be able to meet up with the expenses I would be making while in school.

"Before you get a job, you'd need to understand a lot of things around here, so you don't become a victim."

Those words were deep, they meant a lot, and I was actually expecting them. I've heard and read so much about the racism in the US and how it has continued after it was declared illegal. There is no doubt that race is one thing that permeates every corner of the American society and, spot- on, the original sin of the US is racism. It is in the roots of America's DNA and that means for centuries to come, racism cannot be expunged out of the system. The only problem is what the law is doing about it. Let's not get jumpy quite yet, you'll soon find out how the US justice system handles issues relating to racism and you'll also find out the particular race that gets the brutality of racism. "So, where do we start from?" I asked.

My cousin laughed at me. "Are you really expecting some kind of lectures?" He asked rhetorically. "This is how we are going to do this, I'll take you out with me and show you around. From our interactions with others, you'll get to learn. I'll introduce you to a few people that will also help you when I'm at work. All you have to do is observe, ask questions and learn. But here is what you need to know," my cousin said looking at me with utmost seriousness. "As a Black man in the US, you are condemned by the color of your skin into a suspect class. So, you don't react when you get treated as a suspect in a crime they painted, even though you just got here."

The words accompanying the but sent cold chills down my spine. I stood numb looking at him as every word rephrased itself in my head. He pated my shoulder and asked me not to worry, as long as I don't commit a crime and don't overreact when checked, I'd be fine. We set out and he took me round town. We met a couple of his friends, some were Whites but the majority of them were Blacks. He even had some Nigerian and African friends. It didn't take me long to catch up with things. Within two weeks I was ready to set out on my own. I didn't wait for him to find me a job. I got a job in a cafeteria where I was working six hours a day during my longest shift and five hours during my shortest shift. The pay wasn't enough and I wanted to get another job. Like something I would be doing during my off hours, but I already started applying for admission at the Houston Community College and didn't want to overload my day yet. I knew if I gained the admission, my savings and the money I was making from the job wouldn't be enough to see me through college. I didn't rush into looking for another job, my plan was to make do with what I had until I started college and had seen the number of hours I have for lectures for each day of the week. That would allow me decide the type of job I would look for and the number of hours I would be working each day to meet up with both job and academics and also have some time for myself. This was what I wanted, so I had to be ready for it. If it meant pushing myself harder everyday than I've ever done, I was ready to do it. I wrote to my siblings when I got my first job and told them about Houston and what I was doing at the time. I also told them about my journey from Lagos to Houston and how I met an older woman who reminded me so much of mum with the way she treated me. I shared with them some of my favorite moments so far in Houston and what my plans were. I wrote with so much emotion because I was truly emotional when I was writing to them. I had missed them.

Eventually, I gained admission into Houston Community College to study Criminal Justice. My hopes were high but it still came to as a surprise. I was one step closer to my dreams and that was all that mattered to me at the time. I called the elderly woman and told her the news of my admission into college. She was very excited. She sent me 100 dollars and promised to help me when I needed some help. I was grateful to her and more grateful to God for sending me such a person.

CHAPTER SIX

THERE IS ALWAYS A FIRST TIME

There is always a first time in everything, they say. Here is what it was like for me during my first time to ever board a plane. After the wait and we finally got aboard, I was nervous and naïve, but I tried to put them in check. Well, I didn't quite do well in that. I was fortunate to sit beside an elderly woman. Actually, I was supposed to sit beside a young Lagosian, but the elderly woman asked the young man to take her spot three seats in front of mine. The young man didn't hesitate, she had spoken in Yoruba and though I didn't understand the words, I could tell she wanted his spot beside me. The Yorubas as I have heard and noticed are a very respectful ethnic group. I thought within myself as the boy moved if that was allowed, if we were allowed to seat anywhere we wanted. Well, that wasn't my business anymore and the answer to that question didn't matter. The elderly woman looked at my face and smiled. As the pilot announced that we were about to take off, she held my hand, squeezed it lightly, looked at my face and smiled again. She gave me a nod that said *don't worry, everything would be fine.* She noticed the nervousness on my face and the way I sat inside my seat. It was difficult not to tell it was either my first time flying or I was afraid to fly. I gave up that information with every effort I made to conceal it.

The plane finally took off; I could feel it. I could feel its wheels rolling along the runway. I noticed the plane gradually lifting itself from the ground, I closed my eyes and clenched my teeth. That was it, we had taken off, and we were in the air. I became more nervous as the plane was in the air. I tried not to look out through the window. I was too scared to.

Again the elderly woman squeezed my hand and whispered. "You don't have to be afraid, look out the window and enjoy one last view of your country home." She said as though she knew I wasn't coming back to Nigeria again.

She was right, I told myself before boarding the plane that I would enjoy every bit of the flight, but there was no way I would do that with my eyes closed. I opened my eyes but didn't look in the direction of the window. I kept my head straight and my eyes forward. However, I couldn't deny my side eyes from catching glimpses of the rusted rooftops littered in different clusters.

"You have to enjoy the view while we are still close to the ground."

I looked at her and then managed to look through the window. It wasn't fear that greeted me, it was awe. I was amazed at the view. The rusted rooftops in their different tinges and clusters, the beautiful vegetation in the distance and then some of the high rising points elated my sight. I smiled and looked at the elderly woman again.

"Thank you mama," I said underneath my breath.

"I knew you would love it, son. We all did when we first caught a rare sight of the beautiful endowments nature has blessed us with."

That was it, the view never ended. As we climbed higher into the atmosphere, rooftops gave room for colors in different patches. I could no longer identify what was what. Mama kept me engaged through the flight. We talked about the civil war and the memories that it took away from us and the ones it replaced. She shared with me how she lost her husband and two children and how she and her remaining three children were able to survive after the war. She also shared with me how she got the connection that took her remaining children abroad. She made sure it was never a dull moment through-out the flight. I occasionally looked out through the window and each time I did, the view that greeted me was always nothing but beauty. I wasn't sure if it was the beauty we were flying amidst or the old woman that took it upon herself to make me comfortable throughout the flight that made my flight. Whatever it was, I was definitely enjoying myself. My thoughts drifted to my parents and my siblings. How she was able to notice the flashes of emotions on my face was something that amazed me. Anytime my emotions drifted, I would turn my face to the window and pretend to be looking outside, but I would feel a gentle pat on my shoulders. I would turn and there she was, her old rugged face, which explains at one glance the hustle she's been through, would be beaming at me with smiles.

"I know you miss them, but they are proud of you. And for your siblings at home, they would want you to tell them in detail how this day went."

She always had me with those words. She was very good with words and knew just how to place them. I guess she had had a lot of hearts to sooth in her lifetime. Even though I was enjoying the flight, I was eager to see what Houston looked like, what life was beyond the borders of our national territory. I had the opportunity of meeting some White men back home in Nigeria, but it was always from a distance. Being born at the dawn of the Independence afforded me the opportunity to meet with some of the White men that were administrators in the then eastern region. My joy was, this time, I'll sit among them, walk and work with them, interact with them and also do business with them. I had a lot of plans all locked up in my head. I planned to not only study but explore the opportunities that were available in Houston. I had a nap in the plane for almost two hours. It was one of the most peaceful sleeps I've ever had. I was awoken by the pilot's announcement that we were two hours away from Houston. I felt like I had missed a lot views. Mama also had a nap, but hers was shorter than mine. When I woke up, there she was looking at me with smiles all over her. I wondered in my heart if she ever stopped smiling. Almost like she could read my thoughts, she muttered some words to me.

"When you've lived the life I've lived and led the life I led, you will realize that life is beautiful and it is us who often times don't see it. I've come to a point in my life where happiness is the only drug that keeps me alive."

I knew what she was saying. I remembered the words of my mother, she always told me that there was really no need to worry about life. *Just live your best life, do the right things and you will always be happy.* Always try to make other people happy too and you would be truly happy. Those words then meant nothing to me, but as I grew up and had to take care of things myself I realized worrying didn't get any problem solved. I learnt it was okay to occasionally get worried, but never ever stay worried. I had a lot of lessons playing in my head—the ones I learned by merely observing other people; the ones I learned by listening to adults converse; and the ones I learned from admonitions and conversations with both adults and young guys. The ground in the distance was more beautiful than the one I had left behind at home. All the natural features I had been seeing made me marvel and humbled at the beautiful works of creation. I saw from above the way the lands spread themselves into the oceans and how the waters did not hesitate to swallow them up. The colors of the oceans and the vegetation combined to spark great beauty.

"Nature is beautiful." I muttered while looking out through the window.

"Indeed, and what you have been seeing is just a minute fraction of the beauty of nature."

I imagined what she meant, but I wasn't surprised at all. I always admired the flowers I saw in my home town and the vegetation and small water bodies. However, this I was seeing was nothing short of the biblical creation story. I started seeing a lot of colorful buildings and lights in the distance below. Mama saw my curiosity and told me we were close and already flying over the US. Not long after my observation, the pilot announced that we were an hour away from our destination. Mama smiled at me and told me to hang on that we were almost there. I was relaxed though, but not enough. I was still nervous about the life I was going to meet down there. I was curious to know what was waiting for me down there. Another thing that was on my mind was how the Whites celebrated Christmas. Since I was arriving Houston in December, it was already obvious that I would be greeted by a lot of Christmas preparations and all of that. I've seen some of their movies that were shot during festive periods like Christmas, I've seen how much significance they attach to the season. It was a season of love and I wondered if I would be greeted with love. I heard it wasn't easy for the Blacks in Europe and America. Well, one thing was certain, I was going to find that out just as I found out that flying could be so much fun if you choose to let it be.

Humans are unpredictable, you cannot tell by looks and sometimes even by experience what the behavior of a man would be under a given condition, I thought to myself. Not long the pilot announced that we should all take our seats and brace ourselves that we were going to land in less than ten minutes. I never stopped admiring the sights under me. As our plane descended, the buildings and other structures became more apparent and revealing. I was surprised and amazed at how much the Whites had advanced. We Africans were like centuries behind them.

We descended and unlike the way we took off, this time the head went down while the tail stayed up. I became curious to know if the landing was really that frightening or it was just based on how we described it. I could see some people who were even more nervous than I was, I just wondered if they were also flying for the first time. Mama told me some of them were first time flyers like me, others are those who are afraid to fly but couldn't help it. There were other people who were as calm as mama. I locked eyes with one of such and the young man smiled at me and nodded his head. I got what he was saying, he wanted me to relax and brace myself. I tried to see if I could identify all the first- time flyers on board, but couldn't. There were first timers who were all relaxed like they have been flying all their lives. The landing gears made contact with the runway and soon we were completely on the ground running and gradually coming to a stop. I liked the way the pilots handled the trip. They were perfect. When we finally stopped, mama looked at me and smiled.

"How was that for a first time?"

I smiled at her, —not bad at all."

She laughed and patted my back gently.

CHAPTER SEVEN

LIFE IN COLLEGE

Injustice has a shape, and a weight, and a temperature, and a texture, and a very bad taste.

MJONATHAN FRANZEN

My late mother before her death used to love the way White men carried themselves and commanded so much respect, she admired the

way the educated Nigerians who worked with them were respected and how they went about their jobs. She always wanted us to get western education outside Nigeria, in a White man's land. Nothing else was on my mind. I was both happy and sad. I wore a smiling and happy face in front of people, but when I was alone, I wept. I wept for the fact that my greatest inspiration didn't live to see me become a student of an American college. I imagined how happy she would have been to be part of this day.

It was a dream-come-true when I gained admission into the Houston Community College. When I received the mail that morning, my joy knew no bound. I knew that was the beginning of something bigger.

I started preparing for college. My first day in college wasn't the best for me, but it was just a step in a thousand ones to come. I knew I was in for a lot more than I had imagined. I was expecting some unfair treatments given the kinds of behaviors I had received outside of college. The people in college were products of the same society that gave me those unfair responses. I was only expecting it would be a lot more controlled by the authorities, but then, my expectations were too much. College was a different world entirely. It was a world filled with people of my age bracket and few adults as administrators and teachers. For some kids, it was the fresh air of freedom that they had always craved for. They became like uncaged birds that had been held back for so long and was finally free. They explored all that they saw as opportunities in the environments around them. Some children maintained the standards they had been taught from home. They seemed to understand the system better than the lot of us.

The bad thing about maintaining that standard from home was that, if it was bad from home, it got worse in college. It was worse for fresh year students like us. A lot of them were like wild cards. They were like loose cannons all over the place. I saw a system in the college, a system that was slightly different from what I had seen in the society. Even though the school is a miniature society, there is sometimes a lot of difference between what that precisely means and what people meant when they used the phrase. The moment you walk into college, you will automatically know where you belong. College had a defined structure set in the minds students and their interpretations of the society. There were fraternities and brotherhoods, sisterhoods and all sorts of groups and sub-groups. You will find groups of the high and mighty. I wasn't ready for any categorization, I wanted to be neutral and free of any group, but that was impossible. The system already did a fine job to ensure that college works contrary to the laws of electricity. Here, like charges attracted and unlike charges repelled each other. Even if you don't find your likes, your likes would find you.

I used my first two weeks to understand the system. As a Black boy from a newly independent Black nation, I knew where I belonged and didn't try to cross that line. I learnt from the mistakes I made before gaining admission into college and used them as guide. Even though what I saw wasn't entirely what I had expected, I was still careful enough not to be a victim of an evolving society. I had one goal, and that was to work hard and never let myself be distracted by the events around me.

If there is anything I had learnt from home, it is the power to choose who we would ultimately become. My mom ensured that we did not let the society define who or what we would become. I learnt from how she bounced back from my father's death and raised us with so much happiness. My first year didn't end the way I had wanted it to, but it was good enough to be called a start. Like they say, aim for something great and if you don't hit it, you will end up with something big. I made some friends, they were Blacks too; a fellow Nigerian, a Kenyan and a Black American. We studied together and did virtually everything friends could do together. We kept our heads down and tried not to be noticed by others. It helped us stay focus on our goals. The three of us worked together during assignments and projects except when we were placed in different groups. We shared different rooms in college, but we found a way to always be together. We had something in common. Each of us had a part time job we did after school hours. I maintained my job in the Cafeteria I was working before my admission. I had an agreement with my boss, Mrs. Brown to be excused during my school hours. She agreed to let someone take my shift during my school hours while I took the person's shift. Mrs. Brown is a Black American woman with kids my age. She complained that they never showed up after school to help. When I offered my services, she was glad to find a Black boy with some sense of responsibility.

The job sometimes was quite stressful, but I tried to not always let Mrs. Brown see me as weak. I made more money during the weekends because I had more time to work and even more when I didn't have any major assignment or project. There were weekends I got tips from some Black customers and yes, a particular White American was fond of me and always gave me a one dollar tip anytime he patronized the cafeteria. Mrs. Brown always gave me bonuses during weekends. My friends said that I was fortunate to have found such a boss. They got tips too, but not as much as mine, although they had more supports from their families than I had. We started thinking of how we could invest our savings and make more money and how we could even start a business of our own as college students. The ideas weren't bad, but it would cost us more than just the capital that would be involved; our academics would suffer for it. We may end up with lower grades than we were known for. We decided to drop the idea and focus more on studies, at least for the first year. As time went on, I found the job to be taking more of my time and denying me the time I needed to do other jobs. I had planned to take two to three jobs to enable me meet up with my educational needs. I explained to Mrs. Brown and she understood, she only felt bad that she was going to lose a hardworking young man.

I applied for the job at the factory, then, I looked for another job to complement it. I applied for the delivery job and also got it. I was placed at a time that was convenient for me to work and school. I had two jobs and the salaries were each better than what I was earning while working for Mrs. Brown. I was earning 45 dollars per day. The jobs sometimes were stressful, but I had made up my mind to work so hard.

My friends and I got ourselves study schedules and we were always studying when we were not at work, church or school. We were the typical bookworms. We could practically bury ourselves in books when we were less busy. I had already developed a reading culture, so reading was no longer stressful. That was one very good habit I had brought with me from home; that and working hard. The jobs I was doing were only on week days, I was free throughout the weekends. I didn't like it, so I decided to get myself another work to cover up for the weekends. I eventually got one with a laundry. My services were only during weekends. I had three different jobs and an education to pursue. It was enough for me. Going through school was fun. My first year was tough for me academically. I couldn't meet up with a lot of things, I became an average student. My grades were not the impressive grades of the highflyer I was back home in Nigeria. My cousin told me not to beat myself up.

Coming from an environment considered to be over five decades behind America in development wasn't going to be for me. I was competing with students that were born in the system and raised by the same. They were already used to how things worked and they had high school curricular that was far better than ours in Nigeria. Competing with them would mean I would have to triple my effort. I learnt my lessons from my first year and promised myself my second year would be far better than my first. By the end of the second year in college I was already used to the system. I learnt how to use the technologies and how to make research, I was familiar with the environment and the school system. I was used to the way the society treated people like us, so nothing came to me as a surprise anymore. My grades were better than the first year and I was all set and ready to compete with the top students of the class. There was one obvious thing in my class, the Black students were better than the White academically, although we had more White students doing well. Because of the total number of White students with good grades that was more than the total number of Blacks, it was easy to conclude that White students were better. The top three students were Blacks. In sports, we had more Blacks representing in the school's various sport teams. Music wise, the figure was almost even. Texas is known to have a lot of Black population and a community college like that still had more Blacks in attendance. The Whites went to colleges that were considered more prestigious. We had a lot of points to prove, that was the point for all of us. Maybe most of us. The Black community I found myself part of was trying to prove to the Native Americans that they were not second class citizens and that they were capable of so much more than the society had permitted them. It was a stiff competition in the school. I was glad to be part of that competition: it was something I had always wanted. I had always wanted to be part of a healthy contest, even though sometimes it didn't always turn out to be a healthy one. There were days when the both races would clash against each other. The authorities and the police always favored the White.

I once had an experience with one of the third year student. He claimed I was having a relationship with his girlfriend. Well, I wasn't. We were just classmates who became friends and often time studied together. He confronted me several times with his friends. Good thing I was always in the company of my own friends and we Black folks always looked after our own. I wasn't into the segregation thing, I had seen what segregation could do to a society, but most of the kids probably only read about it. They were very younger than I was, and if it were back home in Nigeria, I would have disciplined them like an older brother. But I was in America, where you are not allowed to fight for your own right as a Black person. The law only recognized your right when you have someone in the top floor of the police department or legal system. I did my best to avoid any physical brow with the young man. I was surprised when he approached me and apologized. I accepted his apology and we became friends. I later found out that his girlfriend explained things to him and he later understood the relationship we had was nothing more than friendship. Kelvin became my first Native American friend. I had met some Native Americans, but none of them were my friends yet. We were just companions and acquaintances. I was happy to have been able to turn a foe into a friend. Not many Blacks liked how it turned out between Kelvin and me. But I never cared, I had a friend and that was all that mattered. After some months, he was accepted into the Black community and that became the beginning of a long term peace. My greatest joy was that my name would always be mentioned among those who did something to let peace reign between both races.

The third year came with its own challenges. It was in my third year in college that I really understood what the statement —the higher you go, the tougher it becomes" really meant. To me it was just another variant way of expressing the geographical principle, the higher you go, the cooler it becomes. What they really meant was the academic work. I thought of dropping one of the jobs I was doing, but when I remembered the bills I had to pay, I just couldn't help but continue with the jobs. I was used to doubling my efforts so as to achieve the result I desired. It was time to double my efforts again. By the time I was done with my third year in school, Kelvin was already a graduate. We went for his graduation ceremony and also had a dinner with his parents later that evening. He introduced us to his parents and they were very pleased to meet us. By the time we were done at his place, it was already late in the night. My cousin would have been worried for my whereabouts, but I already told him I was going to stay back for a friend's graduation party. I had plans of out from my cousin's after graduating from college, we got along quite well, but I felt I was old enough to stay on my own. I told him about my plans and he was okay with it, besides, he was also planning to get married the following year which eventually coincided with the year I would be graduating from college. He has always been a nice guy right from back home in Nigeria. He's one of those I called my favorite family members.

Kelvin had his brother drop me off at home that night. He wanted me to stay over and spend the night at his place, but I already told him I wasn't staying over and since I only told my cousin I would be returning home late, I needed to keep to my word. We went back and forth on it but he eventually agreed. I promised I would make it up to him. I got home and my cousin was already asleep, I didn't disturb him since I had my own key to the front door. I opened and went straight to bed after checking to confirm everything was okay and in their place. I thought about the party as I lay down and some of the new friends I made that night. But the major thing that was on my mind was how mine would be like. It was obvious I wasn't planning to have any party and even if I did, there wouldn't be the family members I would have loved to be around. I considered Kelvin and my other friends to be lucky to have both parents alive. I was an orphan who had to sweat out every step I took. If I had to throw a party, it would be like every other party I've been to, just friends and maybe one or two family members. To me, I never wanted such a party. I've always wanted to celebrate with the remaining of my family members; my two younger siblings and the relatives that have had my back over the years. The last time I got a message from home, my siblings were doing fine. My older brother had a good job in the city while my sister was in her final year in secondary school. So far, they've done well to stay out of trouble. I usually sent them money every six months and I was two months away from my next sending. They usually received the moneys within a period of one to two months after I had sent them.

By now, Kelvin had graduated and so had some of the persons I knew in college. I was in my finals and a quick look at my score board, you'll find I have done so well to keep a good record. At the end of my finals, I finished among the top ten in my class and for me, that was a great feat. The year 1991 brought me very close to my dream. I became a graduate earning for myself an Associate Degree in Criminal Justice in 1991 from the Houston Community College. The run wasn't funny, but I made it. During my final year, I had nursed pursuing a university degree. After graduating college, I applied for a Bachelor of Science program in criminal justice at the University of Houston Downtown. Some people said it wasn't necessary, that I should have just settled for the college degree and make some money before getting a university degree. But I wasn't ready to settle for that—I wanted more. I was eventually accepted. I moved out of my cousin's and closer to the university. I also changed my job and got a better one in Houston.

CHAPTER EIGHT

THE PASSION FOR MORE

It is not possible to found a lasting power upon injustice.
DEMOSTHENES

L earning to me has always been fun and I was ready to keep learning to improve on my abilities and prospects. I was a Black boy from a Black nation still trying to find its place in the new world. If I were to succeed, I needed all the advantages I could get. One of such advantages has always been education. Getting a university degree would obviously up my chances of being hired and eventually succeeding. To us then, education was all for the job. You have to be educated for you to be able to get a well-paying job. The job and the prestige that came with it defined your place in the society. It was a bad ideology, but it was the way of the world. There were entrepreneurs at the time, wealthy ones who changed things without the kind of education I was aiming. But like I said, the orientation of the average African child was to get education and a good job. Taking care of responsibilities was the major reason why we had to go to school as Blacks.

I was beginning to see things differently as I started my university education. I soon realized there was more to going to school than increasing your chances of being hired by the best paying firm. The thought of being an independent fellow was gradually creeping in but hasn't settled in my head at the time. The university was different from the college, but it still had a lot of similarities. The *modus operandi* of the university differed slightly from that of the college. The university wasn't as choking as college. The workloads were tougher, but they were not packed up like college. We were more specific in university. I came across a lot of familiar bodies of knowledge. I was grateful I had a college education in the US before getting this university education, otherwise, there was no way I would have been able to meet up with the academic work.

The teaching and learning methods were more of discovery learning. We were only shown what to look for and a clue to where to look for it. It was completely up to us to discover things for ourselves. I liked the method of learning that made us think out of the box and even as if there was no box. The system was taking us out of the confines of the classroom. We were taking holistic views at things and approaching them from the different points of view available. The aim of this university education was to make us self-sufficient and it was geared towards problem solving. I didn't have as much difficulties as I did with college. Five years already in Houston, I had transformed from that young naïve Nigerian boy from one small village in Abia state. I was now a Black boy in the US with a western certificate and about to get a second degree in the US. That was one thing that gave me respect in Houston. When you are perceived as a hardworking brilliant young person interested in learning, you tend to attract more friendly White people and even the older Black folks. I was loved because I wasn't interested in anything other than work and education. I had no affiliation with any gang which was almost like an occupation for young Black people in the US. I often got harassed by some of the gang members, but I always kept it cool with them, never reported them to the police and never told anyone their identities. I've also been offered different chances to belong to either a fraternity or a gang, but I always turned them down. It saved me a lot of trouble and gave me clean record with the police. I was a law student and I understood the implications of getting in the nest of the police and as a Black boy, it would be terrible for me. That wasn't a path I ever wanted to be associated with, so I stayed clean all the while I was in college and even as I got into the university. I saw young people doing drugs and having their bright future thrown into jail. I saw people at the peak of their academic level and career wasting away in prisons, some losing their jobs and making a shipwreck of their careers. It was a lesson to me and a reason for me to never delve into such path.

The pressure was always there, but in my life I had seen worse. Back home in Nigeria, while I was much younger and had less understanding of things, I told myself never to get involved in anything that was against the law. If I could withstand the tough situation then, I didn't see the burdens I was getting as enough reason to take into anything incriminating. I lost about three class mates in college, two neighbors and a friend to street crimes and drugs. My first year in the university in 1991, three first year students were expelled from school and they were all my class mates. As a matter of fact, it was the passion to fight crime that led me into studying criminal justice. I wanted to be an active participant in healing the world of the fast rising crimes across the globe. There was no way I would be able to do that from a prison cell or with a dented record. I did a lot of community services, went to a lot of public hearings and discussed with a lot of legal practitioners and active officers in the Criminal Justice Department. I learned a lot from them and some of their ideas helped me through school. I focused my research on the relationship between small street crimes and large scale crimes such as bank robberies, serial murders and terrorism. It was a huge project, but I was able to deliver with the support of some of the persons I met at the Department of Criminal Justice, Houston and some of the legal practitioners I met. I successfully completed my university education in 1994 and graduated with a Bachelor of Science Degree in Criminal Justice from the University of Houston, Downtown.

After crossing each milestone, I wrote my family back home and shared my story with them. This time I was better able to take care of myself and also send money to support my siblings back home. They were happy when I told them I had successfully completed my university education and was set for another program. They would have loved for me to come back home, but I had already been offered admission into Texas Southern University, TSU for a graduate program in Public Administration. I had an accumulated 15 credits semester hours. I dropped out of TSU without completing the program and in the same year, I went for a Criminal Justice program with the Police College in the University of Houston Downtown Criminal Justice Center. This was the program that taught me the nitty-gritty of becoming a police officer.

I learnt the arts of making investigation; the step-by-step processes that should not be ignored when making any investigation. I was taught how to follow on a lead and how to handle evidence and witnesses. In the police department, such factors were not treated with levity, they are considered assets that must be well protected. If you rough handle or misplaced any evidence, you will become a subject of investigation. If you compromise a witness before he or she testifies, you may lose your job. I was taught how to handle classified information and how information should be relayed from one desk to the other. The trainings were just too much, but I loved them. During this period, I understood some of the laws I had questioned when I first got into Houston, I saw the reasons behind some of the procedures I was subjected to and why my race was treated the way we were. I only felt bad for some of the reasons. They taught me about the chain of command and how information flows, my job and its relationship with the constitution of the United States as well as every other laws in Houston. I learnt my role as a criminal justice officer as well as my rights. One thing I enjoyed about the program was how detailed it was. Sometimes we were tagged along officers on duty just to learn how it worked out there. We were warned that the field will always be different from the office and the classroom. We should never mistake a real life situation for a symposium. I could remember one day I was a tag along from the school to a rape case. The officer in charge of the case gave me ten minutes to interrogate one of the suspects. It was my first time. Even though I had learned it in school, I was still not sure what to say. I owned up, walked up to the young man in the interrogation room and sat in front of him like his life was in my hands.

I questioned him like I was a pro. At first he was reluctant to answer my questions, he felt like I didn't know what I was doing since he overheard one of the officers saying I was only a tag along. But when he saw that I was a different tag along, he began to spill. I was able to extract information from him that helped us crack down the rapist. I was congratulated and given a reward for a job well done. I maintained a good record each time I was attached to an officer in charge of a case. By the time we were about wrapping up the program, I already got a lot of recommendations from different officers. I could remember one of the officer telling me that he would love to have me on his team. I smiled and said I would also love to be on his team. He was a decorated officer in Houston and Texas as a whole. Officer Bill was one of the officers every junior officer wanted to work under, I was no exception. I also wanted to work with him, but that would depend on if I got hired by the state and posted to work with Officer Bill. I learned a lot while working with him and he knew how to make you reach beyond your limits. There were times I would just go to him for counsel and he always came through for me. I had other officers I went to too and none of them ever disappointed.

I was given some basic training in combat and self-defense. I learned how to use the riffle and how to disarm an assailant. Those drills were stressful but totally worth it. I was taught how to deal with people under different conditions and handle people with mental health conditions. Those trainings were my favorite because they exposed me to the world of human behavior and why people sometimes do the things they do. Even though some persons may not have any particular reasons for acting in certain ways that contravened the law or endangered their lives and those around them, some persons actually do so because their mind at the time tells them to. People with mental health conditions were part of the problems of the society; they often commit crimes unintentionally, they put up deviant behaviors that put their lives and other people's lives at risk. They were difficult to handle because even when you think that they are cool, they could just snap and hurt themselves or someone close. The other categories of people were those who are mentally healthy and physically healthy but have behavioral disorders that make them behave in certain ways. We were trained to handle these people in such a way that they are not threatened because they too have rights and at all point we must seek to respect and protect their rights.

CHAPTER NINE

THE REWARD FOR HARD WORK

Law is a perfect profession in which success can rarely be achieved without some sacrifice of principle. Thus all practicing lawyers – and most others in the profession – will necessarily be imperfect, especially in the eyes of young idealists. There is no perfect justice just as there is no absolute in ethics. But there is perfect injustice and we know it when we see it.

ALAN DERSHOWITZ

One week to completion of the program, I already secured an employment in Harris County Community Supervision as a Probation

Officer. I was happy to take the job and couldn't wait for the last one week of the program to be over. I had high hopes about the job. I've always wanted to be involved in it; to help people lead a better life. My job ranged from managing records of parolee to intervention and supervision, managing cases, being part of court proceedings and conducting general assessments of parolees. My first job once a referral is received was to carry out an assessment on the offender. I would contact the offender and his or her family and also reach out to the law enforcement personnel in charge of the case. I would join the relevant authorities to gather information about the offender's health and lifestyle. It was also my job to also use the information gathered during the assessment to formulate and also document strategies that will help the parolee get better and lead a better life. I was also providing support during court proceedings. I would accompany the parolee to the court and provide support for organizational recommendations for the parolee.

I remember a particular case I was assigned to, a 32-year- old male citizen who was sentenced to jail for 13 years for raping a minor. I helped him got back on his feet. His records showed that he had been arraigned several times for abuse. I recommended that he be placed on a rehabilitation program after finding out that his medical records showed that he has a behavioral disorder. The man was placed on a daily treatment and within six months, he showed great signs of improvement. I was also handling another case within the same period, but this time the young parolee was in for drug and substance abuse. He was also placed in a rehab. Both parolees within one year came clean. There were other cases that involved mental disorders and something traceable to family history. Handling such persons were not entirely easy, but it was a job a deliberately signed up for and as such I didn't have any excuse to give, plus I loved the job. Whenever I was given a case, the first thing I did was to check the person's criminal record and health record, then, I would look at the crime and see if there was a victim. If there was a victim, I would get the necessary permissions to initiate contact with the victim and the victim's family to gather more information.

I made tremendous success as a probation officer with the Harris County Community Supervision. My boss loved me and the way I handled each case. He once told me he wished he had more officers like me. We laughed it off that day and continued on with what we were doing. The only problem I had was the fact that I was a Black man. I got praises but others got the raise and the promotion.

I was very professional with each case and tried not to be emotional about a case. It was part of the training we received. We were trained not to let our personal feelings interfere with a case. It was okay to feel certain way, but never okay to act based on how we feel. At all point our goal was to put lives and the law first. There were times when we found ourselves at crossed roads, such situation we were allowed to act in ways that does not obstruct justice and at the same time does not endanger even the parolees. Of course we knew the consequences of taking laws into our hands, it has led a lot of good officers into prison and made some of them to be dismissed from the police. For every officer, dismissal from the force for careless decisions and mistakes was considered as an embarrassment and shameful way of losing your job. It was worse when you end up behind bars. Hard choices were made at different times, but I was always careful never to let my decisions become the reason I lose my job. My only problem was being emotional. I had let my emotions show in some cases, but I always had a way of putting them under check and not letting them get the better of me.

Every difficult case we cracked attracted a bonus for me. There were times when I helped established a link between a small crime and something bigger. That was thanks to my project during my Bachelor Degree program. I used most of the findings I made then to solve a lot of puzzles. It helped me narrow down problems, and even allowed me ask the relevant questions, connecting all the dots easier than a lot of my colleagues ever did. When cases became difficult, I was always asked to help out. Team work was one thing I enjoyed, as much as I achieved success working alone, my greatest success always came when I worked with people. I had good record with team work, most times, I just listened and did less talking. Sometimes, I was the one doing most of the talking. My background from Nigeria and how I lived through school allowed me to pay attention to details. I never left any stone unturned. My colleagues sometimes would say that I had the perfectionist syndrome; that I always wanted things done perfectly. Yes, they were right. I was the type of officer that would consider all the options I had before choosing a particular option to work with. I was never known to give up. When things didn't work out with a particular option, I didn't just opt for the alternative, I would go back and evaluate the entire process again. Perhaps, we were missing out on some details that were relevant to our course. That perfectionist syndrome was something I inherited from my late mother, it followed me from home and it helped me a lot. Although, there were times when it delayed the process and almost got me into trouble with some of my colleagues and with some families. Somehow, I always managed to avert the problems. I knew when I was being too careful and when I needed to discontinue on a path.

Two years later I decided to change the category of people I want to be dealing with. I later cross-trained as a Juvenile Probation Officer with the Serious Offender Supervision Division. It was a state grant program. I loved the job so much as I was exposed to a much younger set of offenders. I got the chance to interact with young adults with serious criminal records. For some of them I felt enormous pity for them, while some were directly responsible for their predicaments. Some of the adolescents grew up with a single parent who barely had time for them, they had to work out certain things on their own. They got wrong counsels and ended up making the wrong decisions that landed them in juvenile prisons. There were some of them that grew up under the roof of parents who have been arrested several times for one criminal offence or the other. Such kids had a lot of difficulties becoming who they wanted to be. Listening to these kids sometimes make me so emotional. I imagined what life was like for them. I could relate with a lot of their stories because I was almost raised by a parent, except I lost mine before I knew my right from wrong. My story was harder than a lot of theirs, but we had different environments and what was permitted in Nigeria was not permitted in the US. I shared my stories with some of them and used it to encourage them. For some, it worked while others just said I was lucky. I hated it when they tried to make excuses for their failures. At their ages I was already taking care of extra mouths, something none of them could ever do at the time.

During my time as a Juvenile Probation Officer, I had two very interesting cases that filled me with so much surprise. The first was a young girl who was going to be 18 years three months after the time her case was brought to us. At the time we received the case and my boss instructed that I supervised her, she was pregnant. It wasn't the pregnancy that got me shocked, teenage pregnancy was a common story in the US. I wasn't surprised that she got pregnant before she was 18. I was surprised that she was pregnant for her fifth child at the time. As her supervisor, I went through her records found that she has all five babies from different fathers. I was shocked to learn that. But just when I thought I was done getting surprised information about her, her records showed that she actually started getting pregnant at the age of 12. That was something that took me quite some time to absorb. I tried to imagine how a 12- year-old girl could successfully carry a child and have a safe delivery. Apparently, she was one of those girls who experienced early puberty and she also got wrong information and ended up confiding in the wrong persons. She had little or no knowledge about menstruation and when she experienced hers, she went to the wrong persons for advice because her parents at the time didn't have her time. She was one of those kids from a broken home.

It was common in the US to have kids from broken homes turn out like that. Some have voids in them that their single parents couldn't fill and so they resulted to habits that caused them more than they could carry. The girl in question had her first child at age 12 and at the age of 14 she had another. As she turned 15, she was already pregnant for a third child, seventeen she had her fourth and just before she turned 18, she was pregnant for her fifth child. We had to subject her to a lot of treatments considering the time she started giving birth and the intervals between each birth. It was too much for a girl her age and something that might leave her permanently damaged. I helped her through the process of her healing and she actually got better emotionally and mentally. That was the first time I was seeing such situation—I only heard.

The second case followed two months after the young girl's case. But this time it wasn't about procreating life, it was about destroying existing life. I have had to deal with cases of rape, but never from a boy as young as 13. Yes, I once had a case of a fifteen years old boy raping a thirteen years old girl. This time, this thirteen years old boy actually raped his 2-year-old niece. Now he committed the rape crime not just once, but enough to get the little kid infected and enough to cost her life. The young boy's story was saddening; he had lost his single mother while he was yet 13. He had an older sister who had 4 kids and were all under the supervision of the Texas Child Protective Service because of neglect that resulted from the use of drugs. The authorities decided to make his older sister his legal guardian. His sister's youngest child was a 2-year-old girl. Disappointingly, the young boy raped his 2-year-old niece. The crime was committed several times for some days. The little girl caught an infection and was taken to the Harris County Hospital. Sadly, she died some days later. An investigation was conducted as to the cause of her infection and then they found that she was raped severally by her uncle which got her infected. He was certified as an adult and his case was treated as a case of an adult. The judge gave a final verdict that saw the boy sentenced to life imprisonment.

I was really touched by the young boy's sentence, but he was a murderer and the law doesn't take kindly with such crimes. We did all we could to ensure that the boy turns a new leaf while in prison. There were other cases but these two cases really had me. Every officer that heard about the cases wondered what was becoming of the younger generation.

CHAPTER TEN

LOVE AT LAST

They say what shall be shall be. I couldn't believe my eyes when I saw my long lost friend Ezinne from Ogbor-Hill, Aba. She was in the hospital one day when we brought a young boy with a gunshot wound for treatment. She was carrying a file and heading into the theatre. I was sure I had seen a familiar face, but I didn't call out to her yet because of the emergency condition of the young boy. I waited until she came out.

"Ezi" I called out with surprise written all over my face.

She stopped abruptly hearing the familiar voice and how it sounded with typical Igbo accent. It reminded her of me. She turned and looked at me. She was even more surprised than I was. I stood looking at her with a feeling of surprise laced with joy. We dashed towards each other and hugged ourselves with so much excitement. The other nurses and families just looked at us with mixed feelings. She introduced me to her colleagues and I did the same. We decided to go out together that evening after she had closed to catch up on the other. I could swear that I had found love. We went out on a date that evening and shared each other's stories and that night ignited more passion than I had ever felt. She was a licensed nurse at the time and was working in the hospital we met. We started dating and in six months I proposed to her and she said yes. We got married two months after I proposed to her and that was the beginning of my family life. We now have 4 children together, 2 girls and 2 boys and a girl I had from my first girl-friend in Houston Texas before I met her.

My kids grew up into good and loving children. They all had passion for learning and at the early age of 6, each of them already made a choice of what they wanted to study in the university. We encouraged them all along and gave them the support they all needed. They were always among the best in their classes. They would run home to tell my wife and me how they were honored in school. Each of them knew how to make us happy. We loved them so much and were willing to do anything to make them happy.

I could remember when my first girl got sick, how we had to run around to make sure she was fine. My wife as a nurse was even more worried than I was at the time, but just like me, she learned how not to let her emotions interfere with her job. She played her role as a mother and a nurse but allowed the professional doctors to do their job. She eventually got better and we were very happy. The problem she had was it affected her academic performance for that period. She was behind her class mates and couldn't put in the extra efforts she needed to meet up. That period she fell from the top five in her class to the top ten. She wasn't happy with the result but we had to encourage her she was good given her health condition. My other kids during this time were all worried for their sister. When she came back home, they all volunteered to help her do some of the things she was supposed to do. They took the older sister's role from her until she was strong enough to be the Ada of the family. She had her father's blood, she was ready earlier than we all imagined.

My children grew up to become successful and for that, I am very thankful to God. Despite everything we went through together and what they went through on their own, they still came out very successful. My first child took the path of her mother and graduated with a Bachelor of Nursing degree (BSN). It was a thing of joy at home. She went further to pursue an advance degree in Nursing. The second girl completed B.Sc. in Biology and went ahead to pursue a career in pharmacy. She will be graduating in May 2019 with a Doctor of Pharmacy Degree. Our third daughter is a 19-year-old first year student in the university. Our first boy graduated in May 2018 with Doctor of Pharmacy degree. He sat for his Board of Pharmacy Exam and passed very well and now working in the University of Texas Galveston facility. While our second boy graduated with BS, Electrical Engineering on December 14, 2018 and already had a job offer with USAA. It was unfortunate that they achieved all of these without both of their parents.

I was living my American dream and that was one of the best feelings I ever had. When I look at my family and the story that brought me to the US, I can only make one conclusion regarding all of it; —the wisdom of God, the Divine Providence, the Will of God rules the world" this realization/understanding, conviction/recognition opened the gate to my perpetual joyful activity to the honor and my personal recognition of God the only One, the Almighty.

CHAPTER ELEVEN

THE ENTREPRENEUR

Injustice anywhere is a threat to justice everywhere.
MARTIN LUTHER KING JR.

Not long after I got married I started putting my entrepreneurial mind out. I decided to try out something different from paid employment. I knew I had always wanted to be self-reliant and own my own business. I shared with my wife my intentions and she bought into the idea. She gave me some advice and I also got some from other entrepreneurs I knew. The number of small businesses I founded and co-owned ranged from store- front, ecommerce, transportation to healthcare service. My first business was a store front. I decided to retail some household appliances. I got into the market and made my research; I researched about my potential customers and my competitors and also the products I was planning to sell. The first year in the business wasn't so bad and it wasn't so good. I was told not to worry that the first year of every business is considered the seed year. They even told me I was lucky to not have incurred some loses during my first year. They were right, I made some profits but it wasn't enough to make me want to remain in the business. By the first half of the second year, I was making reasonable profit and I was grateful that I didn't give up after the year. I continued with the business for another three years before I decided to do something else. I went into ecommerce. It was fun and interesting for me, but it wasn't my field. I struggled a lot in ecommerce and wasn't really happy. The money was good, but compared to the effort and sacrifices I was putting in, I didn't see it as worth it. I was giving too much and getting too little. Also, considering the fact that I wasn't really happy in the ecommerce industry, I wanted to try something different. I was only waiting for the right time and I was still searching for the next type of business to start. I attended business summits and conferences and a lot of things about the entrepreneur's journey.

In one of the conferences I attended, one of the speakers said — succeeding with your first try doesn't really prove that you are an entrepreneur, but when you fail and still bounce back stronger and better, then, you can consider yourself an entrepreneur." Those words meant a lot to me at the time. I was beginning to regret why I quit my job as a Juvenile Probation officer to go into entrepreneurship. After that conference I found a new business idea. I decided to go into transportation services. I didn't have enough capital to go into the business alone, so I partnered with someone I met at the conference. He was thrilled by the idea. We were going to get some cars and use them for transportation. The problem was we didn't have enough money to buy the number of cars that would be required to drive home a reasonable profit. We sat down and brainstormed on how we would go about it. Eventually I got the idea of getting people's cars and putting it out for transport services and sharing the returns with the owners of the cars. The idea was good. There were lots of families in Texas that had cars that they no longer used. They probably belonged to a late loved one or they just got tired of the car after they bought a better one. Some of the cars had minor faults that they were not ready to fix since they have alternatives. We registered our business name and drafted all the necessary papers regarding our partnership and those of the car owners. We set out and contacted families with cars they were no longer using and would want us to use.

A lot of families bought into the idea as they felt the car would be more useful out there than in the garage. Some families didn't like the terms of agreement we presented to them, while some were happy and willing to go on with the idea. We had a category of people that were indifferent with the idea. They wanted to try out the idea and see if it would work. We had a target of starting with 20 cars and using that to test-run our idea. When we had the required number, we were good to go. The first three months was good and our clients and other partners liked the idea. We decided to increase the number of cars from 20 to 40. Doubling the number was good, it brought in the kind of returns we wanted. We started having challenges when we increased the number of cars from 40 to 60. The drivers we had were no longer trust worthy. Maintenance became a problem and clients began to complain. The business only lasted two years. I pulled out of the business to save me the embarrassment that was looming. We got sued three times for making clients miss their appointments, another four suits for over speeding. The last suit that made me backed out of the business was one that related to drugs. I hated to be mentioned whenever a crime that related with drugs was concerned. I had kept a clean record since my arrival in Texas, I didn't want someone else's crime to drag me into the mud. I sold my own shares to my partner and used the money to start a different business. I went into health care services and that became the last business I went into.

The healthcare services became a turning point in my whole entrepreneurial journey. Before jumping into the business, I made a lot of research. I took some time to analyze my market and competitors and the industry at large. I was going into something that has always been in a high demand in the world over, there was no way I was going to succeed in the healthcare industry if I did not equip myself with more than just the necessary knowledge. The healthcare industry over the years has always been a highly competitive one and one that the government does not joke with. I had tried saving lives as an officer, now I was going to try save lives as a healthcare practitioner. My family loved the new business idea since I already had a wife in that industry and my children were aspiring to be healthcare practitioners. I developed my first plans and strategies to achieve my plans. My plans included the things I needed to do before starting the business, the things I needed to have before getting a business space, the persons I needed to work with me, my marketing strategy and the way I would go about the services. I also included in my plans periodic evaluation of the process we would be making. Tracking and monitoring of progress was part of each phase in my plan.

It was time I updated myself with how things worked in the industry. I had no basic training in the health sector other than the few tips we got while I was in the police college. I went for basic training in healthcare services and how to run a healthcare firm. This was a different field from the ones I had previously been involved in and I couldn't afford to make mistakes as that might cost the life of a client. There were lots of areas when it comes to the healthcare sector. I learned about handling clients' information and what the industry consider as Protected Health Information and the Healthcare Insurance and Private Policy Act (HIPPA). After my information gathering phase I decided to kick start the business proper. I got the necessary licenses and all the papers that I needed. I went ahead to acquire the equipment I needed and also got myself a business space. I evaluated the steps so far and made the necessary adjustments before moving on to the next phase.

I began the next phase of the business which was hiring of personnel to work with me. As soon as I had the necessary personnel to work with, I proceeded to the marketing my business. I was set for business and I needed to start selling. In my marketing phase I used a proprietary method —paid referral," which was a marketing strategy that I developed by myself from my research. I used the strategy and it turned out to be a good strategy. I was very successful with strategy. I got clients faster than I had projected. My marketing strategy wasn't just successful, it made a lot of other competitors nosy about my business. They said I was too new in the system to have such a ground breaking growth rate. Most of those who questioned my strategies were the conservationist old healthcare providers. They didn't believe in the reality of my strategy. I explained it to some of my colleagues that were close to me, while some understood the marketing strategy, others didn't. The old conservationist colleagues argued that I was a novice in the system and a new comer. That was their problem. They didn't believe that a Black man with no background in health would be able to record that level of success within a short period of time. I recorded exponential growth with my strategy; it was faster than anyone had ever recorded in Houston and Texas. My wife told me that there were lots of people making comments about my strategies and the comments were not pleasant. She was worried that something was going to be happy. Other colleagues were beginning to report to the law that I was using an illegal means to lure their clients from them and gradually kicking them out of business.

He was right. A close friend of mine in the force told me that they have been receiving reports against me and the government had begun investigating my business. According to him, it wouldn't be long before they found something to use against me. I wanted to slow down things a little or even stop. But if I dared to slow down or even stop, that would make it easier for them to crack me. They would conclude that I was slowing down because I noticed the way people were being concerned about the business and the dust I was beginning to raise. If I stopped, they would say I stopped because I wanted to cover something. They always have something to say that would trap you in their net. I was there once, I use to think like that too, I knew how they crack down on people. I wasn't about to play into their net. I knew it that once they start looking into you, they wouldn't stop until they have been able to find evidence that puts you down or they on their found that you are innocent. In this case I knew I was innocent and even if they scheme up something, I would be able to take care of that in the court of law. I had nothing to hide and wasn't afraid to go to court. I called my lawyer and told him what was going on, he knew it that it wouldn't be long before they come to arrest me. He told me that we needed to start preparing for a case. I never thought one day I would become a center of attention by some powers that be or even the law. I shared the development with my wife and children. I kept the details from them but I let them know that something bad was coming. When I started receiving more information about how much the law was caving in on me I decided to let my family know how bad things could get and also let them know that I was innocent.

I tried to picture out the angle they would be coming from, but I couldn't find one. I was very sure I had tightened every loosed ends and dotted all my I's and crossed all T's.

Eventually they finally showed up. It took them long enough to knock on my front door and I knew what that meant. They had finally found an angle to come at me. I was only hoping that I wasn't about to become another victim of racism; a Black boy rising so fast in the US always attracted all sorts of attentions.

CHAPTER TWELVE

NOSE DIVE

In matters of truth and justice, there is no difference between large and small problems, for issues concerning the treatment of people are all the same. We are not to simply bandage the wounds of victims beneath the wheels of injustice, we are to drive a spoke into the wheel itself.

DIETRICH BONHOEFFER

The nature of the charges was life-altering before the grand jury. If I had gotten an appearance as a bystander before the grand jury it would have made a world of difference. Also, considering the fact that this was my very first time to be involved in a crime at all with the criminal justice system at the age of fifty-three then, I was expecting the law to be considerate. People were always given considerations when they are involved in any crime at all for the first time. Even young adults were given considerations, but not my wife and me. This was clearly a conspiracy. There were people who wanted me out of the way because my spouse and I were their biggest competitors in the health care services in Houston. We had registered our business legally at the time as Family Healthcare Group, Inc. and incorporated it as minority owned small business in the state of Texas. We were in good standing with the TDAS and were also licensed and certified as a healthcare agency by TDAS. The way we were treated was ridiculous because we were a licensed and certified healthcare service provider. We had even passed the Medicare and Medicaid Stringent Survey Guidelines, including private insurance such as Evercare, etc.

Before we began operation we were checked thoroughly and each of our service areas which included skilled nursing care, durable medical equipment DME, and personal care with over 50 employees. My spouse was temporarily employed as the director of nurse from June 2006 to October 2, 2008. Both my spouse and I officially resigned our appointments from family healthcare group, Inc. effective October 2, 2008. During these periods we had no report against us and we were never involved directly or indirectly in any fraudulent acts. We kept a clean professional record with the healthcare group. I know I counseled a lot of other younger healthcare practitioners on how to keep a clean record and avoid the law clamping on them. I never knew that I would be facing such grave crime in 2009. We felt really bad with the way the system was treating us.

After we resigned from Family Healthcare Inc., my co- owner, Mr. Prince, became the sole-owner of Family Healthcare group, Inc. Before my spouse and I resigned, I already started my own healthcare service firm. I started Special Healthcare, Inc., got the necessary licenses hoping that I would be able to operate and own the newly licensed agency with my spouse and other employees. We made all the necessary changes and had them confirm and authorize per Texas Secretary of State. The Texas Secretary of State before issuing a confirmation and authorization checked our previous records and found that we had kept clean records both as citizens and as healthcare service providers. We eventually started operating the Special Healthcare, Inc. We were in operation for 20 months before the scandal. Within that period of 20 months, we made a gross profit of 2 million US dollars. It was all there in the documents that we presented to the FBI, but it seemed not even a confirmation and authorization certificate from the Texas Secretary of State could clear us. We were too deeply in it. I knew there was no way I would win with the turn things were taking. I decided with the little knowledge of the justice system that I had that I was going to hire a legal counsel to represent me in the court. I went ahead.

I hired the law firm of Scardino & Fazel on July 30, 2009. They did what they could, but they were not yielding any positive result. I wasn't satisfied with the kind of progress they were making. It was like we were roaming in cycles. We did endless paper works with them, made endless phone calls and had ourselves worked out on regular bases. My kids were all worried, it affected their academics. They were mocked and bullied in school and even denied certain privileges. I would return home tired and exhausted each day. The Special Healthcare, Inc. was shutdown. We were spending money on the case. I was only happy that my kids were grown a little to understand what was going on around them. They knew we were innocent. They knew they were just another victim of a failed and biased system. Each time we made an appearance in court, my counsel was unable to prove any tangible point that would help me get free. Each appearance we made only sent me closer to prison. I was largely unsatisfied that I was spending money and not getting results. Apparently, my counsel was only interested in the money he was making from me.

About seven months after I hired Cardino & Fazel, I decided to look for a different counsel to represent me. I started interviewing other attorneys for hire. On March 8, 2010 I hired a new attorney, A. Fisch and on March 9, 2010 he filed a motion to the court to become my attorney of record and start preparing for my defense given his past defense experience in similar cases. He had a good track record and experience with such a case which was good for us. A case like ours required someone with as much experience as possible to be able to face this bias court and agency. He told me that the agency through the court would offer me a plea deal. If I accepted, I would be pleading guilty to a crime I didn't commit and it would mean that I would have a criminal record. He advised me not to accept any plea deal less than acquittal, the case was against the company, Family Healthcare Group, Inc., that allegedly violated the Civil Monetary Penalties Law provisions applicable to physician self-referrals, Kickbacks, False and Fraudulent Claims. As a result, Family Healthcare Group, Inc. will have to settle it as self-disclose conduct to OIG and agreed to pay back the amount as charged. His advice proved that he knew what he was doing. I agreed and when I was offered a plea deal other than acquittal, I refused the deal. That day I saw the look on the face of the prosecuting counsel and the judge. So I knew something was fishy. There was something about their demeanor that suggested to me that they knew what was going on and they wanted me to walk right into it. When I didn't accept the plea deal, they looked somewhat frustrated that their first attempt at convicting me with less effort had failed.

The greediness of my first attorney and the denial of my second attorney by the court to legally represent me pushed me into making some findings. I made some researches on the OIG top-false and fraudulent claims archive and found that there were 134 Healthcare companies that allegedly violated the Civil Monetary Penalties Law provisions applicable to physician self-referrals, Kickbacks, False and Fraudulent Claims from April 15, 2008 to June 22, 2011. It was surprising that none of the companies in question and cases were criminally prosecuted. What the OIG did was to settle these cases as self-disclosed conduct to OIG and agreed to pay back (their companies) the amount as charged by their companies. On the other hand, for the same violation my spouse and I were criminally prosecuted and incarcerated, two worlds in one country. The companies that walked away with their crimes were either owned by the White Americans or co-owned by a White American.

CHAPTER THIRTEEN

IT ONLY GOT WORSE

Little thieves are hanged but great ones escape.

I was shocked to hear that my new attorney's motion to become my attorney of record was denied. The denial came the day after he motioned to be my

attorney of record. He immediately informed me not to worry, that it was just a matter of procedure. He told me that he was going to send another motion to the court for reconsideration. I had little knowledge of court procedures, so, I stopped meeting with my old counsel and continued to meet with Fisch for updates including other actors around him as indicated in the retainer agreement.

On March 23, 2010, two Washington, DC prosecutors, S. Sheldon and C. Reed, communicated to my former attorney, A. Fazel, who was no longer in on my case with a plea offer. I saw that as a waste of time. I said to myself that *this can't happen*. I called it fake news or conspiracy because I already rejected a plea deal when it was suggested by the prosecuting counsel. My concern was why would they send a plea deal to the attorney I no longer wanted and already fired and not send such offer to my new attorney, A. Fisch? I wondered how the plea deal would get to me to officially respond to it. The other time I rejected the plea deal, it came as a suggestion which I responded to swiftly, waving the idea off the table. To tell you how this whole thing was cooked up, they went ahead and sent it to my old attorney. They deliberately rejected my new attorney's motion to be my attorney of record because they knew he was not going to accept the deal. The offer states, if I accept the offer, an additional case involving my spouse for her activity in Family Healthcare Group, Inc., where she had a brief stint of employment as director of nurse would not be filed. I ignored it without actually receiving it directly or indirectly. Regardless, I had been advised by the incoming attorney not to accept any plea deal that was short of acquittal. The deal itself was more of a conspiracy, they were smoking me out using my spouse as the bait. They know well enough that I would like to keep my wife out of the case so they painted up the offer as a deal.

Almost three months passed in a case of this magnitude and I was without any attorney of record. It got me disturbed and wondering how I was ever going to swim passed this legal river without a counsel. I asked myself why the federal judge would not allow my new attorney to represent me. I have the right to an attorney of my choosing and I hired and paid him to represent me in court in this very case because he proved and demonstrated to me that he had the experience and skill to successfully get me acquittal. I didn't understand what was going on, I really wish I did. There were lots of questions on my mind and there was no one to answer or should I say no one was giving me the kind of answers I needed. I talked to some of my old colleagues in the police and even they too were surprised at the turn the case was taking. They were surprised that the case had taken such a long time. I really didn't know what else to do. I kept on communicating with Fisch and hoping that he would eventually be allowed in on the case. Meanwhile, all these while, my former attorney did not even approach me with the deal that was sent to him. I wondered what he did with it and if he had the right to respond on my behalf.

When I started asking more questions and demanded before the court to know what was going on, someone then gave me privy information. According to the source, there were two branches of the Department of Justice in Houston that was prosecuting and investigating my new attorney A. Fisch and I respectively. We had the Washington prosecutors (S. Sheldon & C. Reed) prosecuting my case, while the Department of Justice Branch in Houston (Johnson) were also investigating the new attorney. I was hoping that a case such as this would have an effective and efficient channel of communication between the two DOJs involved. Sadly, Communication and coordination between these two branches were nothing but poor. This made matters worse for my spouse and me. It literally multiplied and complicated my problem unnecessarily. The agencies were breaking all of the rules and getting away with them. They were eavesdropping on us and bugging us. They sometimes tapped into our conversations. There was an occasion when the prosecutor wired other defendants and they listened and intercepted our attorney-client conversation. It was that bad. This, in an ideal system, was a complete violation of our rights and considering the fact that we were not found guilty of any crime yet gave them no right to have done such thing. I wondered if that was the new *modus operandi* of the agency or it was because they were dealing with an African- American family of Nigerian descent.

I was told there were other charges that would be filed against me if I failed to accept the plea deal. I paid no attention. I took it as a threat and a way of making me accept their plea deal. I was sure that I was innocent and accepting the plea deal would mean that I was guilty. I was head-bent on not accepting the deal. On June 2, 2010, the two prosecutors carried out their threat, they filed an additional charge against me. The new case involved my spouse and me and also included others on superseding indictment. It became two separate cases from one and in two courts with two judges respectively. I had case number H-10-416 and H-09-421 in two different courts and judges, same charges in both courts. Confused and surprised as I was, I contacted my new attorney to alert him and at the same time seek for his advice especially now that my spouse had been indicted along with me in the superseding indictment. His only response was to file another motion for reconsideration and wait. I was tired of waiting but I literally had no choice. I could see the injustice in the system already, the words of Walter Savage Landor, —delay of justice is injustice," played in my head, but I had no choice but to wait still.

It was bad enough that they had denied his motion to be my attorney of record when we had one case, but now that the case had become more complicated, I was hoping that the court would reconsider their initial stand and allow him represent me in court. Unfortunately, the court denied his motion for reconsideration. That did not stop him, he continued to ask for my patience to enable him file a writ to the Fifth Circuit Court of Appeal that will force the lower court to allow him become my attorney of record. Fisch also told me that it was my constitutional right to choose my own attorney to represent me, as long as the attorney of my choice is qualified, not disbarred. While all these went on, I had no official legal representation or counsel and did not know why the two courts and judges failed to respect a defendant's right to a counsel of his own choosing. Deprivation of a defendant's right to counsel, or denial of a choice of attorney without good cause, should result in the reversal of the defendant's conviction, according to the U.S. Supreme Court. They knew this and somehow still denied the motion. I wondered if I could file a suit against the judge for denying me my right to an attorney of my choosing. I didn't have the resources to pull such tight strings and even if I did, I still needed an attorney to do that, and that would increase the number of cases that I have to three. There was no way I would be able to meet up with all of that. We were approaching the date we were supposed to make an appearance in court and there was no defense counsel. I wondered if the court session would proceed with a defense counsel, or perhaps the court had the intentions of forcing my former attorney on me and making him represent me.

CHAPTER FOURTEEN

THE UNJUST VERDICTS

There is no greater tyranny than that which is perpetrated under the shield of the law and in the name of justice.
CHARLES-LOUIS DE SECONDAT

There is also a painful story of injustice recorded in the United States system. 46 years ago, a teenage boy named Wilbert Jones was wrongly accused of

rape. Not a single shred of physical evidence existed to prove his guilt. He also had an alibi witness proving he was somewhere else. He had nothing to do with it. Nothing at all. In fact, a serial rapist who had victimized another woman a few weeks later was the perpetrator. And the local police and prosecutors had evidence of this, but decided to keep it to themselves. A full three months after the crime, the police couched the victim into identifying Wilbert as the man who raped her.

And the jury convicted Wilbert Jones, a young teenager, for a horrible crime that he did not commit. From 1971 on, Wilbert suffered through an unthinkable prison sentence. Think about this: when he was convicted, it was just two years after the assassination of the then President. And all through the 70s, 80s, 90s and 2000s until 2017, Wilbert Jones was in prison. He practically spent a large part of his adulthood behind the bars. For the record, Jones is Black and poor, he was convicted after a trial lasting a few hours. On one uncertain eyewitness's testimony, he was sent away for the rest of his life. The 30 freed clients (except one) under Innocence Project New Orleans were like Jones, young Black men, when they were arrested and convicted at trials that lasted less than one day. We know African- Americans are disproportionately represented among the exoneree population nationwide. We should tend to ask why we accept cursory and inaccurate process for the poor and Black people. Here is where the divide sets in.

Although the police investigated the rape for which Wilbert was convicted by waiting for a name and putting him in a lineup. When the victim called the police to say she wasn't certain it was him, they did nothing more, but he eventually spent over 16 000 days in prison for a crime he did not commit. There we see a lot of matter arising. Why the police or the enforcement agents are not given adequate resources to conduct an effective and thorough investigation. Also, to enable them with modern best practices in eyewitness identification procedures. We should ask the question about the value placed on the lives we ruin completely when people are wrongly imprisoned. The height of it all is that it essentially paints a broken legal system.

Another tragedy was the death of Kalief Browder who was just 22 years of age. Unfortunately, Kalief Spent three years in jail without ever being convicted of the crime with which he was charged. Kalief's story is one that is of a great concern to not just his family, but the entire community of New York at large. The whole event about his conviction and death clearly depicts a deeply broken justice system in the States. The system that punishes people due to the fact that they are poor and helpless and eventually subject individuals to coldhearted and brutal dealings. Kalief was arrested in 2010. As at that time, he was just 16 years of age and was basically accused of stealing a backpack. Also, he was charged on robbery, grand larceny and assault. His bail was set at $3 000. At that period, the family could not afford that the amount. Consequently, Kalief didn't get to go home after he was charged. Instead, he was sent to jail in the same New York City. All this was because he was wrongly accused and he could not afford to pay a huge amount of $3 000.

Unfortunately, Kalief spent more than 1 100 days incarcerated, maintaining his innocence throughout. Prosecutors repeatedly offered plea deals, which Kalief rejected. After 74 days of incarceration, bail was revoked altogether. Moreover, this poor boy was falsely and unjustly accused of stealing.

> *Acts of injustice done between the setting and*
> *rising sun in history lie like bones, each one.*
> W.H. AUDEN

Finally, it was the day to make an appearance in court and I still had not counsel to represent me as the case was with attorney of my choosing and the court has not been resolved. I decided to find an alternative. I was allowed to make a temporal arrangement. I retained a different attorney, Fry, for one court arraignment. And on September 14, 2010, I retained another attorney Alston under serious pressure and hoped this attorney would be able to meet with the prosecutors and negotiate back the plea offer that was made earlier. I was hoping to forestall an event where two parents, my spouse and I, would face prosecution at the same time. I found myself at a crossroad. If I didn't take the deal and I couldn't get a counsel to help me win the case, I would be in for something bigger. My wife and I would both serve jail terms leaving my kids all alone by themselves. It would be bad for them to have a parent as a convict and even worse to have both as convicts. I felt like the world has remembered my sins. I had my whole life's story from my country home in Nigerian playing like a movie before me. I reached out to the contacts I had and, still, nothing happened. There was only one way I would be able to do something to prevent both of us from getting jail terms. The deal. The deal was my only card at the time. If I couldn't save myself, then I should save my wife the defacing reproach of being called a convict. I needed someone to take care of my kids, even though they were no longer kids, they still needed the help of their parents.

When one has been threatened with great injustice,
one accepts a smaller as a favor.
JANE WELSH CARLYLE

I took the step I had refused to take for some months now, I agreed to plead guilty to an offense I did not actually commit considering the nature and circumstance surrounding the entire case, for the sake to save my family from dual prosecution of both parents. I was afraid of leaving our young and vulnerable children to fend for themselves without any other family member in Houston and in the entire United States.

On September 29, 2010, less than two weeks with the new hired attorney, Alston, without good understanding of the case and what I was getting in return if I agreed to the guilty plea, he rushed the whole process through. He made no serious attempt to retrieve the first deal offer. For a case of this magnitude and its far-reaching consequences on my life and family, a gap of three months without an attorney and adequate representation presented an opportunity for the hungry prosecutors to force-feed me with a plea bargain that was worse than a conviction as events later revealed under my legal counsel's watch. His action brings into question why a prospective defendant will knowingly and willingly accept a plea offer that goes contrary to his own interest thereby making his worst nightmare a realty? The new deal offer was worse than the first deal. As a matter of fact, there was no deal at all.

I didn't stop making my own personal research. I later made another important evidentiary discovery in a document I found from the State of Texas Secretary of State through Business Incorporation Department. The evidence was an official record in document showing the actual date my spouse and I resigned from Family Healthcare Group, Inc. 20 months before the alleged offense for which I and my wife were being arraigned in court over. This document was not discovered and was not presented to the court during the proceedings. With the newly found evidence, it became obvious most of what happened in Family Healthcare group, Inc. occurred when my spouse and I had already resigned from the company.

I immediately compiled my discoveries into a single document and sent it to the presiding judge Atlas by- passing my attorney, two days before my sentencing. The judge took time to examine the documents after which the Judge wondered the type of lawyer that was representing me. The FBI also investigated Special Healthcare, Inc., the new agency my spouse and I owned and operated for 20 months after our resignation from Family Healthcare. After thorough investigation by the bureau on our operation and activity in Special Healthcare for the past 20 months, they did not find any wrong doing or fraudulent activity. Their findings and conclusion were supposed to speak clearly to every fair-minded persons or agency that my spouse and I still respected the law and will not engage in any criminal activity no matter what. But when that didn't happen, I drew my conclusion that the system is bias, particularly, the people who operated it.

On that day in court after it became obvious that I was going to jail, my heart became heavy. I wondered how many years I would be spending behind bars and thought about what would become of my family during the periods that I'd be in prison. The Judge openly stated in court during my sentencing that if today's court appearance was not for my sentencing that she would have given another defense lawyer. The judge said all she could do at that point was to accept my new findings and evidence under-oath as part of my court file recording in case I decide to appeal the case in future. She added that my former attorney Fisch had serious effect on the outcome of the case but cannot do anything now to correct the situation because it remains only an allegation until he was tried and convicted. Not until then. The judge further in her opinion per sentencing stated that —If I were to give a personal opinion on the matter, I would say I sensed some form of injustice in the system and it was only bad that Mr. and Mrs. Clifford Ubani were subjected to the case." She further stated that there is an injustice because Mr. Fisch said or did what's been alleged. From her words, I deduced something she didn't want to be quoted for in a later date. There was something she wanted to change but didn't have the power to. Her actions and words suggested to me that she knew more than she said but was only there to deliver her verdict.

My experience with the justice system can only be described as a tumultuous whirlwind of confusion as I was —speeded and pleaded" and sentenced to 108 and 87 months in prison concurrently. To make the situation worse and more difficult for my family and I, my wife was also convicted and sentenced to 97 months in prison leaving our five young and vulnerable children to fend for themselves. It wasn't just the sentencing that broke my heart, it was the effect it would have on my wife. My wife had been a registered nurse for 20 years and throughout in active practice, she was without any criminal records and had a very good employment history. Her sentencing meant that she now had a permanent criminal record and she would have to forfeit her nursing license. That was like throwing away all that she had worked for and built from high school to her 20 years in practice to something she knew nothing about. It was really an injustice and the agency knew what they were doing. What I didn't know was why they were doing that to us. For me I was ready to serve my term, I wasn't broken by my sentencing, I definitely knew I would be sentenced to jail. It was my family that mattered most to me. The system paid no attention to my days as a probation officer, the records I made and the awards I got then while in active service. In an ideal society, they would consider our track records as individuals and as healthcare practitioners. I was also expecting that they would consider that that was the first time we were ever having anything to do with any crime.

My children broke down into tears. All these while, my co- owner of the family healthcare, Inc., Mr. Prince was also tried and sentenced to prison alongside his wife for the same crimes I and my wife were charged with. I called Kelvin and other persons that I could trust and asked them to help me look after my kids. My cousin had moved away from the US and so had mama. They were the two persons under whose care I would have gladly left my children.

On October 19, 2010, a twenty-one count of federal indictment was filed against attorney Fisch and others for alleged conspiracy, obstruction of justice, and etc., indictment case H-11-722. Several events occurred under my nose. At a point I wondered if I was just a pun in a bigger game. I was not aware that at approximately the same time that one of the Department of Justice in Washington D.C. represented by Mr. Sheldon and Reed were busy prosecuting my case, another branch of the Department of Justice, the United States Attorney Office in Houston was also investigating my attorney Fisch, and others for defrauding criminal defendants. During their investigation, conversation with Fisch and others were intercepted. Rob was the prosecutor, my spouse and I debriefed with him couple of times concerning our involvement with attorney Fisch and others. As this was going on, the DOJ and its other branch were not communicating with each other, it invariably affected their decision-making and the outcome of our case. The lack of communication between both prosecutors was highly unprofessional. I was going to jail for two different trials and served two different jail term. It was horrible and disdainful that a court of that magnitude could not effectively do their job. Well, they refused to communicate with each other so that they would have enough excuse to carry out their mischief.

CHAPTER FIFTEEN

THE INCOMPLETE TRUTH

Man cannot be freed by the same injustice that enslaved it.
PIERCE BROWN

Fisch's trial was not concluded until around June 2015. During this time attorney Fisch was tried and convicted as alleged, per judge Atlas's comment as contained in the sentencing record, it's sad Mr. & Mrs. Clifford Ubani, they're innocent, not guilty. That statement made a lot of difference. I was already in jail for four years- plus. My wife too. The trial of attorney Fisch opened a new way for my family and me. I was informed in jail that Fisch was sentenced to prison and the presiding judge actually stated that I was innocent. I was very happy because such a statement would go very far to help my family and me.

One question I kept asking myself was every state in the U.S. and provinces in Canada had some form of client protection fund. In Texas, this fund is called the Client Security Fund and it holds more than $3 million in its corpus. Payouts are funded through an annual appropriation from the Bar; interest on the corpus; and any restitution received. Applications to the Fund are reviewed and acted upon by the Client Security Fund Subcommittee, a standing subcommittee of the State Bar's Board of Directors. The CDC through Claire Reynolds serves as the administrator and legal counsel to the Fund and Reynolds is responsible for conducting investigations on applications and presenting recommendations to the Subcommittee.

Unless the lawyer is already disbarred, resigned in lieu of discipline, or deceased, eligible applicants must file a grievance which results in findings that the lawyer stole the client's money, or failed to refund an unearned fee. Applicants must present proof of their losses, and meet the statute of limitations for the Fund, which is 18 months following the date of the disciplinary judgment.

I made my application for this client security fund, knowing very well that I was qualified to receive this fund. I paid my attorney $50, 000 who is a member of the state bar of Texas. The court did not allow him to represent me and did not give me any reason, later the lawyer was indicted, tried, convicted and sentenced to prison for a separate and unrelated case. When I applied for this client security fund, they told me that I was qualified to receive it since I went to prison without him representing me in court, instead he committed a crime and is now in prison. Why shouldn't I get the $50, 000 I paid the attorney from client security fund which it was for? It's simple, because I am different, a Black man of Nigerian decent, people who operate the client security fund are bias.

The wheels of justice caught up with my personal attorney in the case, he was indicted by federal prosecutors in a separate but related case and one of the cases cited as part and parcel of his legal sins was my case 4:10-CR-00416-001. This was the case for which he was tried and convicted. This brings us to the famous legal analogy of the fruits of a poisoned tree. If my personal attorney's legal sins were steeped in scarlet and legally unforgivable, then he represents a poisoned tree and everything he touched legally is considered contaminated. The defendants he touched and cases he handled are all deemed contaminated and as such, subject to be set-aside by the virtue of legal ethics and practice. I was a victim of a filing system. My case was attached to my personal attorney, yet I was convicted four years before the time the truly guilty person was tried and found guilty. It meant I was coming out of prison. I wondered if I would get compensated for the treatment given to my family and me. Even though the wheel of justice could not turn fast enough for me to escape spending time in prison, it should have benefited my spouse to stay out of prison but it did not. I was also hoping that this divine intervention, justice and fair play should have demanded that my spouse should not be denied of the divine favor by providence.

After my former attorney Fisch was found guilty as alleged and sent to prison, I was returned to court on writ after spending 65 months of the original 108 months in prison and was released to freedom. During this court appearance, the presiding judge had been replaced by another who knew little or nothing about the case. An opportunity that would have helped to remind the judge about the comment the first judge had made, about our innocence, if Fisch was found guilty as charged. The system and the player knew the implication of that statement and they knew it would have automatically wiped the board clean for my wife and me. But the players in the whole controversial scandal refused for once to connect the dots. They blatantly refused to let the new presiding judge know what was said. I wondered if that was erased from the record that was given to the new presiding judge. The unwillingness of the justice system and its operators to make this link or connect the dots to my spouse's serving a staggering sentence in prison kept me wondering if I was the target or my wife was. I wondered if I was actually the one they wanted out of their way or if they were particularly targeting my wife and whether I was the only link to getting her. I was freed from prison and, but my wife still remains in prison till date. For her to get out of prison as I did, I need to hire a lawyer and file a motion to the court asking the court to re-open her file and then wait. So, I need a lawyer and money to do it which I don't have at the moment.

As I regained my freedom, I imagined everyday what my children were going through without us. I knew even though we were innocent, the fact that we were in prison and my wife is still in prison would always be used as a stigma against them. My girls were quite emotional like their mother, but my boys had my kind of heart. My former partner, Mr. Prince, remains in prison till date. His wife was released to freedom earlier before me.

While in prison, I never gave up on my marketing strategy. I knew I wasn't in prison because of the strategy, I was in prison because of a failed system. The four years I spent in prison for the first time in my entire life should not be in vain, it afforded me the opportunity to engage in more research, reviews and fine-turned —paid referral" marketing model to —Peer-to-Peer" Referral Reward Contribution combined with subscription business model to rewardingly monetize, engage and enhance users' experience across social networking platforms. Now I wish to put this business model that has worked for me before, in a more refined way to better users' experience in social networking platforms around the world. I started teaching it to more persons who were willing to learn.

In the beginning there was only a small amount of injustice abroad in the world, but everyone who came afterwards added their own portion, always thinking it was very small and unimportant, and look where we have ended up today.
PAULO COELHO

ABOUT THE AUTHOR

Clifford Ubani is a successful entrepreneur and author who is of Nigerian descent. He first graduated from Houston Community College with an Associate Degree in Criminal Justice in 1991, before going on to study at the University of Houston, where he added a Bachelor of Science Degree in Criminal Justice three years later.

Since then Clifford has also attended the Police College in Houston and it is probably fair to say he has had his fair share of the law during the course of his life. He is married and he and his wife have five children; 3 girls and 2 boys.

Clifford's entanglements and experiences with the law has led to many feelings of injustice and discrimination. Through it all he struggled to keep his family together and on the right tracks while dealing with a society that appeared to operate two distinct sets of laws; one that depends on who you are and the color of your skin and the other which doesn't.

Now Clifford has put all of these thoughts into his book *The Wheel of Justice*, which tells of his incredible fight every, step of the way in his life, against a system that did not want to see him succeed.

In his spare time, Clifford enjoys writing, relaxing and spending time with his family and friends. He is rightly proud of his achievements and those of his family, who have all managed to carve off their own piece of the American dream, despite the odds they faced, and he hopes that his book will inspire others to succeed where it seems hopeless.

www.ingramcontent.com/pod-product-compliance
Lightning Source LLC
Chambersburg PA
CBHW022059210326
41520CB00046B/715